My Old Man

My Old Man

Tales of Our Fathers

Edited by
T E D   K E S S L E R

CANONGATE
Edinburgh · London

Published in Great Britain in 2016 by Canongate Books Ltd,
14 High Street, Edinburgh EH1 1TE

www.canongate.tv

1

British Library Cataloguing-in-Publication Data
A catalogue record for this book is available on
request from the British Library

ISBN 978 1 78211 398 0

Typeset in Goudy by Palimpsest Book Production Ltd,
Falkirk, Stirlingshire

Printed and bound in Great Britain by Clays Ltd, St Ives plc.

CONTENTS

In the beginning there was a song, 'My Old Man', sung by Ian Dury and written about his father, William George Dury. It was released in 1977 and has been in the back of our minds ever since. It goes like this:

My Old Man
by Ian Dury and The Blockheads

My old man wore three-piece whistles
He was never home for long
Drove a bus for London Transport
He knew where he belonged
Number 18 down to Euston
Double decker move along
Double decker move along
My old man

Later on he drove a Roller
Chauffeuring for foreign men
Dropped his aitches on occasion
Said 'Cor Blimey!' now and then
Did the crossword in the *Standard*
At the airport in the rain
At the airport in the rain
My old man

Wouldn't ever let his guv'nors
Call him 'Billy', he was proud
Personal reasons make a difference
His last boss was allowed
Perhaps he had to keep his distance
Made a racket when he rowed
Made a racket when he rowed
My old man
My old man

My old man was fairly handsome
He smoked too many cigs
Lived in one room in Victoria
He was tidy in his digs
Had to have an operation
When his ulcer got too big
When his ulcer got too big
My old man

Seven years went out the window
We met as one to one
Died before we'd done much talking
Relations had begun
All the while we thought about each other
All the best mate from your son
All the best mate from your son
My old man
My old man

CAN BIRTHDAYS STILL BE HAPPY AFTER AN EIGHTIETH?

Felix Kessler by Ted Kessler

My Old Man began as a blog in 2013. I had Ian Dury's gently melancholic song of the same name in mind at the time, along with two other ideas. First, a quote from Milan Kundera's *The Unbearable Lightness of Being*. 'We can never know what to want,' wrote Kundera, 'because, living only one life, we can neither compare it with our previous lives nor perfect it in our lives to come.' Hot damn, that cut me in two when I read it pulled out of context on the jacket flap of another book. I never know what I want. I always think there's some great experience, or party, that I've accidentally opted out of by choosing a different path. Maybe there was a way of comparing notes.

Also in my mind was my own father, Felix, who was about to turn eighty. It seemed an epic age for anybody to become and there was to be a rare family gathering to celebrate this in Paris, home to my middle brother Mark, his wife and kids.

As the day in May approached, I brooded. Could birthdays still be happy after an eightieth? I kept thinking about the shadows that the passage of time cast and how my dad, at his stage of the game, embodied some of my queries about time's flight.

When we're young, and if we're lucky, our idiosyncrasies add nuance and mysterious shape to our selves. They give us edge. But as life progresses, those quirks fossilise and warp our personalities into a permanently awkward shape. What may have seemed unique, hip, even, to a younger entourage curdles over the years. By the time middle age is standing in the hallway hysterically ringing its bell, those characteristics are ending marriages and making weekly appointments with a counsellor. If we survive long enough to become a question mark for our children, our nearest and dearest acknowledge those same USPs by rolling their eyes and making cuckoo signs behind our backs. It's the cycle of life. Your must-have value just diminishes.

That night in Paris I had a lot of that on my mind. On the way to dinner I remembered the intense, pensive man I mainly saw only in charismatic glimpses growing up: head wrapped in bandages after a car crash in Egypt; standing knee-deep in seawater, one hand behind his back, reading, for hours; breaking 100 mph in the driving-seat during explosive in-car rows with my mother; inventing complex bedtime stories about the mystically gifted Squeaky the Mouse; typing furiously through the night at the living-room table, predicting my own future. I contrasted that man with the gently eccentric old moose of today, pottering around New York doing his dry-cleaning in the spring and tending his yard in Florida in winter. Which period of his existence does he feel best represented by?

On the night of his birthday I wanted to fast forward through

2

the chit-chat and get right into it with him. As usual, the opposite happened. I couldn't find the space to pin him down, choking on the pathos as we all sat in a darkened bistro, cupping our ears and chinking our glasses.

So, obviously, I wrote something on the Internet about him when I got home instead. Others, encouraged by my fearlessness, followed suit and, as the site gathered more contributions, I realised that, despite dominating my interior for so long, my own paternal story was really a very minor drama. There were sons and daughters writing about how their fathers had abandoned them as babies on My Old Man, about cruel and violent men, about those whipped away by dehumanising illness just as life was motoring, about frauds and thieves, about coming home to find their father swinging dead from the bathroom door frame. Really, how bad had my story been? I'd been lucky.

My dad was a complex but always loving, generous father. He moved my family out of central London to suburban Paris for work just as my teens dawned, which at the time seemed cruel to me. I was hormonal, exceedingly English and ill-prepared for the vastness of the change. France was hostile both on the streets and in my enormous school, where I pretended I'd read Le Grand Meaulnes in the barest pidgin French to the audible disgust of my teachers. I was so homesick that when Felix surprisingly announced he was leaving us, soon after he'd deposited us in our strange model new town a million miles from anywhere, I was relieved. My now emotionally distracted mother was such a liberal parent that I knew I'd be able to do exactly what I wanted – i.e. all the things teenage boys dream of but generally don't get away with.

So, there were a couple of difficult years at the start of my teens. Big deal. There followed years of unbridled hedonism and freedom. I was able to leave home and school exactly when I wanted (much too soon) and by the time I was seventeen I

3

was living it up back in swinging London on my own as my brothers, too young to leave home, struggled through another new beginning in Washington DC with my mother as she foraged for independence and work. What did I have to complain about?

In 1988, three years after I'd returned to London, Felix provided an important coda to this story on a sunny pavement outside a New York café. He'd picked me up from the airport and insisted he needed to talk to me before I did anything else. Okay, I thought. Maybe he's going to drop some money on me, away from my girlfriend, who was sleeping at the apartment. Nice. Or maybe he's dying.

'Teddy, I need to tell you something,' he began nervously. Here we go.

'I have a girlfriend, whom I love very much.'

The clarifying relief rushed through me like a hit of ecstasy. 'Great,' I replied. About time!

'And we have a beautiful little girl together.'

Woah, that was quick.

'She's called Gabriella and she's eight years old.'

Even my rudimentary maths could work out that Gaby, my lovely sister, was born shortly after we arrived in Paris and had therefore been conceived before we moved. So that would explain why Felix had spent so much time after we emigrated 'working in Belgium'. His girlfriend, Jair, lived in central Paris at the time and he'd been running a two-family operation. Complicated. Especially when you're a hotshot foreign correspondent for the *Wall Street Journal*, trying to keep the job on track in a competitive bureau when both eyes were not on that ball. I looked at the guy in a whole new light. I almost admired him for it.

Everyone freaked out for a little while over that news, but in time it all worked out for the best. At the time of writing, some twenty-eight years later, my father and Jair remain a married couple. My mother later found a much more suitable, devoted husband, Jim, with whom she lived happily for years before dying suddenly in 2013. And my brothers, Gaby and I, well, we're all right too.

Just as I was editing the last contributions to this book, my old man coincidentally announced he was coming to London the week before its deadline. He wanted to hang out with me and my family before going on to Paris to visit my brother and Gaby, who also lives there. He did the same thing last year and it felt, once again, like his European farewell tour. He's eighty-two and I always wonder if this will be the last time I see him. Let's make the most of it, I vow.

But how? As my dad's grown older, conversation with him has become smaller. Not because any faculties are diminishing. It's simply that he seems less interested in heading anywhere difficult. The waters are very still. Once, around 2009, I accidentally made him cry in the stairwell of his apartment block, so frustrated had I become by his inability to talk about his feelings. 'What do you want from me, Teddy? I cannot be sorry any more than I am!' It wasn't what I was after and I felt dreadful.

Elsewhere in this book Dorian Lynskey writes powerfully about all the conversations he wishes he could have now with his dead father. I feel guilty because I can have them with mine, but I'm no longer sure what the big topics are. We all want to live painlessly for ever – I don't need to make him beg for it. I wondered what we could do together that would have meaning.

I checked the football fixtures. In March 1976, my dad had, on a whim, wrapped me up in too many layers and taken me to see QPR play Wolves at Loftus Road, Shepherd's Bush, near to Paddington where we lived. This small act of curiosity on his behalf inadvertently triggered a lifelong obsession in my seven-year-old self that has determined everything from the timing of holidays to the suitability of romantic partners. When my marriage was breaking up, a relationship counsellor suggested that my domestically unpopular determination to go weekly to QPR was linked to that perfect moment of felicity, when the floodlit blues and whites, gold and black danced upon the electric-green grass, exploding in technicolour in my mind – it was the one thing of pure, abstract pleasure I ever did alone with my old man and I was constantly trying to head back there. I didn't entirely buy it, but I used it on the way to the exit all the same.

But it is my end of that thread that tugs, not his. Not all fundamental memories are two-way streets, it seems. Sometimes, when I'm telling a coat hanger to fuck off or scrolling through my phone distractedly at the soft-play centre, I catch the bewildered look on the faces of my two small children and wonder how they'll remember me. As a whimsical pal, perhaps, full of hilarious anecdote and insight, or will it be as a perpetually distracted wage slave, simmering in quiet desperation? What will their strongest memories of me be? I'd like to think it's of us skipping down Nightingale Lane together after park playtime. But maybe it'll be me punching the wall over a text relaying a last-minute defeat. And in thirty-five years, what will my eldest force me to endure in a bid to make us reconnect?

In 2015, as we sat near our old seats in the Ellerslie Road Stand, watching the modern QPR huff and puff against MK Dons, a team that didn't even exist when my dad last came to a match, I knew it wasn't going to unlock anything in Felix. He stoically delivered the blank smile of clock-watching sufferance throughout. What did I expect? He'd done his best.

After a final dinner, I walked him back to his hotel around the corner from our too-small-for-dads house.

'So . . .' he began, with a sly, cautious smile, '. . . anything you want to talk about?'

I didn't know what to say. So much and so little, and we had about five hundred yards to go. I left it hanging there.

'Oh,' he said, as a diversion. 'I brought you a shirt which I forgot to give you. What size are you?'

'Medium,' I replied.

'It's a large. Let me tell you why I brought you a large . . .'

'Dad,' I barked testily, embarrassingly losing my temper, 'I don't want to talk about the shirt you brought me that doesn't fit me and that you've forgotten to give me.'

Why is my temper so short with him? I don't know. We walked on in excruciating silence.

At the crossroads before his hotel, I let him go. As we waited for the lights, we hugged and I gave him a kiss. 'Love you, Dad,' I said. I really meant it.

I watched him cross the street, his stride still rolling, like that of the jazzy hipster I remember from my youth.

'Bye, Dad!' I shouted.

'Bye, Teddy!' he called back, with a wave, and then that same closed-mouth Kessler smile we share. I wonder when I'll see it again.

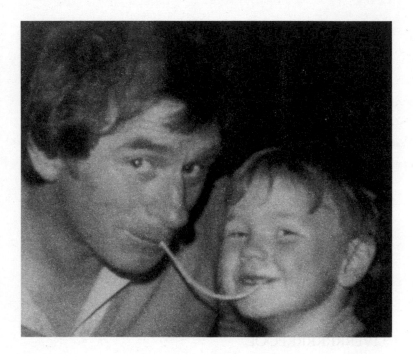

'STARE AT THEM, NICK. THEY DON'T LIKE IT!'

Johnny Ball by Nick Ball

Wednesday, 7 January 2004. It's cold. We are stood outside Stamford Bridge's Matthew Harding Stand as my friend Dan hands us our tickets, Chelsea vs Liverpool. Big game.

'You know that where you're sat you can't support Liverpool, right? Or you'll get lynched.' We both nod in agreement and head off to our seats.

As soon as we sit down Dad stands up, arms out, and shouts, 'LIVERRRRRRRPOOL.'

I grab his elbow. 'Dad, what are you doing?'

'I'm a sixty-five-year-old man. What possible harm can I do?'

As the game begins so do the dirty looks.

It's a feisty opening few minutes: both teams have chances and now the fans behind us are waving twenty-pound notes and chanting, 'WE'RE FACKIN' LOADED, DA, DA, DA, DA, DA, DA, WE'RE FACKIN' LOADED, DA, DA, DA, DA, DA.'

I can see in Dad's face that he's irritated by it – it's the swearing: we're sat next to some young kids and he doesn't think this use of language is appropriate. On the Kop, growing up, it was always witty and fun. It had a sense of humour – he's proud of that: it's part of what being a Liverpool fan is.

The game is close and still nil–nil. Next up from the Chelsea repertoire is the classic 'YOU ARE SHIT, YOU ARE SHIT, YOU ARE SHIT, YOU ARE SHIT'.

My dad can't help himself. I try to stop him by putting my hand on his arm but it's no good. Instead I pretend it isn't happening, I try to focus on the game but I can't: I'm listening. He turns and addresses the bank of lads directly behind us. 'I don't mind you waving your twenty-pound notes and singing about being loaded, at least that has a modicum of wit, but *You are shit?* How is that clever or funny or witty? And there are kids here. What message are you sending out?'

Oh, fuck, fuck, fuck, fuck, fuck, I'm thinking, as I hear the reactions, like a wave passing up the bank.

'It's fackin' Johnny Boll.'

'Look fackin' ell it's only bloody Johnny Boll.'

'Johnny Boll just told us off for swearin'.'

'Fackin' Johnny Boll off the telly don't like me swearin', you fackin' what?!'

I can hear this guy's mind exploding.

Somehow – perhaps it's the shock, the sheer temerity of it, perhaps it's because on the whole he's universally loved, the eccentric, crazy, funny one off the TV who impossibly got everyone into maths and science by dressing up as Archimedes and fooling around, the classroom prankster, but a clever adult version who knows stuff – I don't know exactly why but they let this interruption slide, this impudence; it doesn't kick off. Not yet.

I breathe a sigh of relief while thinking, The balls on this guy. (I shouldn't have been surprised. Years before, at Old Trafford, when Michael Owen was sent off, we caught the eye of a group of United fans. 'Stare at them, Nick. They don't like it!' Dad said. 'STARE AT THEM? THEY DON'T LIKE IT?' ARE YOU CRAZY?). Dad smiles at me, a smile that says, 'That's them told,' and then I hear it. The next chant up. The same but different. 'YOU ARE RUBBISH, YOU ARE RUBBISH, YOU ARE RUBBISH,' and then, 'WE'RE REALLY LOADED, DA, DA, DA, DA, DA, WE'RE REALLY LOADED.' I dare to glance back at the sniggering faces looking down on us, so pleased with their swear-less chants. Just get to half-time, I think. If we can just make it to half-time, it'll calm down.

And then – BOSH! Bruno Cheyrou buries one for Liverpool and we're both out of our seats.

We sit back down but things aren't the same any more. The Chelsea fans are livid. It's no longer funny that the clever fella off the telly told them off for swearing. All goodwill has been eclipsed by the massive unavoidable fact that there are two Scouse fans among them. This will not stand. There will be no more swear-less chanting. 'OUT, OUT, OUT, OUT, OUT, OUT' is the call now, their faces twisted and thick, furious gargoyles, features bulging, fingers pointing. It spreads upwards fast, Borg-like, assimilating the vacant minds of fans who are so far away they can have no idea why they suddenly find themselves shouting, 'OUT,' repeatedly. The hive mind in full effect.

And now furiously rotund stewards in hi-vis jackets are pointing at me, and shouting the same thing. I turn to Dad, who is ignoring the hate, trying to watch the game, oblivious. 'We're being thrown out, Dad.'

'I'm not moving,' he says. And he repeats his mantra, 'I'm a sixty-five-year-old man. What possible harm can I do?'

11

The stewards are coming down both ends of our aisle, faces like smashed crabs. They're gesticulating angrily at me while the fans behind us shout far worse things than just 'Out.' With the stewards almost upon us I stand up, resigned to my fate, and a flicker of disappointment passes across my dad's face. I wonder how he had seen this ending. Actual physical violence is seconds away. 'Well, I'll see you later, then, Dad . . .' I say.

He reluctantly stands too and begins remonstrating with the steward as we're shown to the door. But now the gob is raining down on me, gloopy saliva slamming into the back of my head. The abuse is horrific. Dog's abuse. Those kids are learning some new words today, I think. Dad is ahead of me now, impervious, no doubt repeating his mantra to the uncaring steward. I feel like I'm in *Midnight Express* or any of those prison movies. Just focus on the exit, I tell myself, the perimeter fence. It's close but very far away, a glowing light, freedom. Everything is in slow motion. If I can just make it to the exit, make it to the light . . .

Stay on target. Blinkers on. I'm covered in spittle but I'm nearly there. Just as I'm out I feel a hand on my shoulder and I'm yanked back in. 'I HOPE YOU BREAK YOUR NECK ON THE STAIRS, YOU SCOUSE CUNT!' An old swollen cab-driver type is screaming this into my face with such vitriol, his mouth so wide that I wonder if he's going to swallow me whole. I pull myself clear and fly down the steps to safety. I find Dad going bonkers, repeating his 'I'M SIXTY-FIVE' mantra over and over. We're shown to a tiny poster that apparently says there's to be no away support here. The adrenalin is ripping through me, the rush so strong I can't focus on the words. We're hauled off to the exit. Game over.

But just as we're walking through the door the steward turns, his face curious, as though a light just got switched on in a derelict house. 'Eh, I know you, you're Johnny Ball off the telly, I love your stuff. Think of a what's-it-called and all that. You're the reason I'm where I am today!' Dad and I share a look, eyebrows raised. "Ere, I'll get you in the away end.'

So we're ushered into the Liverpool end where Dad recounts our ordeal to a growing audience of adoring Liverpool fans. 'Get these boys a beer,' someone shouts, and we're handed pints. Heroes back from war. As he tells our story I can see from their faces what they're all thinking: THE FUCKING BALLS ON THIS GUY.

Nick Ball is a screenwriter. He lives in west London with his wife and two kids.

HE'S THE FIRST OF MY MOTHER'S LOVERS NOT TO HAVE A SERIOUS FLAW

Mr Holt by Nina Stibbe

My stepdad came into our lives in 1974 and, as happens in all the best stories, we almost mistook our hero for a villain.

These days, he is known as Mr Holt, the name I gave him in my novel, *Man at the Helm* (and again in my next one, *Paradise Lodge*), and I'm calling him Mr Holt here, too, because he doesn't much enjoy the spotlight. I chose the name Mr Holt for the fictional him because it's strong and straightforward and it's the name of a market town on the King's Lynn to Cromer road, close to where he grew up and where he went to borrow library books. He was the only child of working-class parents, Harry and Ethel, and it seemed right to acknowledge his geography, his Norfolk accent never having left him (or ceased to amoose us).

As a boy, Mr Holt loved school and had a huge appetite for learning, but long spells off sick with bouts of asthma – so

15

bad at times that he'd be rushed to Cromer Hospital in the doctor's car – resulted in his failing the 11–plus. Had Mr Holt passed his 11-plus he would likely have been recognised as the exceptionally bright boy he was and might even have been considered for a grammar-school scholarship. Instead he was put into the lowest classes at Wells-next-the-Sea Secondary Modern with all the pupils labelled 'dunce'. It must have been demoralising, but his parents had brought him up not to think too highly of himself, and he accepted this with no argument.

Over the next couple of years, though, health permitting, he'd cycle over to Holt Library, some eleven miles away, to stock up on books. His avid reading helped him work his way up to the top classes, but by then it was too late for him to consider staying on at school. In any case, his parents wouldn't have entertained it. He left school, like his parents had, at fifteen and went to work full-time in Mr Dale's grocery shop in the village, where he wore khaki overalls and sometimes made bicycle deliveries. His mother and father (a cleaner and a gardener at the grand Blakeney Hotel) were quietly pleased with this outcome, especially since so many others had landed up on the dole.

Around this time, in the Midlands, my mother was at boarding school and, like other girls of her ilk, doing her utmost to get up the nose of her form mistress – and, hopefully, even expelled. Like Mr Holt she was clever and curious and, as with him, higher education was never an option (in her case for reasons of gender rather than class). Instead she was coaxed into a 'good' marriage before she was twenty. It produced four children, one after another, and lasted just six years. And though the divorce was amicable, and she'd started out full of vim, the reality of being a divorcee at that time, in the English countryside, was unbearable. It turned her from fun-loving and adventurous to lonely and depressed, and soon she was dependent on the pills prescribed by at least two doctors, washed down with whisky.

Her mother, who might have been a support, was bitter and disappointed by the divorce. 'No man will take you on with four children,' she said, 'and no woman will befriend you without one.'

In my novel, Mr Holt, a disciplined and intelligent man with no airs and graces, falls for my (fictional) mother (a posh, alcoholic divorcee, fallen on hard times) when she appears for an interview at the laundry he manages.

It was the same in real life. Mr Holt had worked his way up via various organisations across East Anglia and the Midlands, including the delightfully named Maypole Dairy Company, and had landed, in 1974, at Initial Towel Supplies (now Initial Services), Leicester branch, where he managed the staff.

At this time, my mother was looking for work. Her four children were aged between twelve and eight. The family business had gone bust in a national recession, and because she'd accepted shares in the business in lieu of maintenance, she was now broke. She answered an advertisement in the *Leicester Mercury* for van drivers, and Mr Holt interviewed her for a job. He thought her eccentric, interesting and probably trouble, but since no one else applied – certainly no one who was used to driving a vehicle the size of Initial's Leyland vans – he'd had no option but to offer her a test drive. She was a very good driver (she'd driven horseboxes and trailers to horse events throughout the Midlands for years), she could read a map, and was a quick learner when it came to changing the towel machines. Despite her foul language, she passed with flying colours. Mr Holt became my mother's boss and she began servicing the roller towels in public toilets across the county. She disliked the job and the boss intensely. 'The boss doesn't like me,' she'd tell us at home. 'He picks on me. He doesn't think I'm good at the job.'

And it was true: he had serious concerns about her. Of course he did. She drove like a maniac, parked illegally, had a habit of holding the van on the clutch bite and ran around in flip-flops or bare feet. She smoked and ate ice cream at the wheel, listened to cassettes on a portable player and drove with the sliding doors open. She was rebellious, careless, late and, frankly, didn't seem quite 'with it' on occasions. And she'd been known to race along the A6 with drivers from a rival laundry.

Mr Holt spoke to her frequently about the above and she'd apologise sullenly, then try to let off steam to her new colleagues. They weren't having any of it: 'He's a fair boss,' they'd say. So she'd leave the depot, seething, and get it off her chest at home. We adored our mother: we didn't want her going off driving a van and leaving us on our own, and found it all too easy to believe the boss was all the things she said. A stickler, a pain in the fucking neck (we said 'neck' in those day, not 'arse'), a blot on her daily landscape and a fly in the ointment. The names got worse. He was that eagle-eyed tyrant, that miserable fucking bastard and that total cunt. As far as we were concerned, he'd ruined our lives, first by employing her and then by being so consistently mean and picky.

My mother and Mr Holt, for all their differences, couldn't ignore the fact that they were essentially on the same wavelength and they started going out for the occasional drink after work, then discovered a common love of cricket, books and a sense of the absurd.

And she stopped calling him so many awful names at home. In my novel, as in real life, Mr Holt is the first of my mother's lovers not to have a serious flaw (like being nineteen, or married,

18

or gay, or a conman, or a teacher) and that must have felt wonderful to my mother. 'Turns out he's quite a nice bloke,' she said one day, then told us she'd invited him round for dinner.

When he arrived, we couldn't believe our eyes. We'd been expecting Blakey from *On the Buses* but he looked more like Hannibal Heyes from *Alias Smith and Jones*. We continued to be suspicious, though, especially as he clearly wasn't *au fait* with spaghetti and chopped his into little pieces rather than doing the spiralling-on-the-fork thing that any fool knew. He came for dinner again, and this time tucked expertly into a casserole, albeit with a biro behind his ear. And the next time, *he* did the cooking (introducing us to the Fray Bentos pie).

Over the next few visits Mr Holt really lived up to some of the names our mother used to call him. He suggested forcefully, in his brusque manner, that we might help with the washing-up, polish our shoes, tidy up and so forth. Then, just when we were fed up to the back teeth of him, he fixed our little telly by changing the fuse, and told us it was never broken in the first place. When he did the same with a lamp, we began to change our minds about him. He helped us when one of our dogs died, and we saw suddenly that he cared for our mother in a way we'd never seen before. It was such a lovely thing that we knew we could never let him go. I worried that he'd find out what a druggy she was and begged her to tell him ASAP.

'Does he know about all your stuff?' I asked. 'Because he won't like it.'

And she told me to mind my own business and I told her it *was* my business, if she was going to shack up with, then scare away, the only decent man in Leicester. Better to be upfront, I thought.

One night he took her to visit his bedsit in a less nice part of Leicester. She'd been mithering to see it for romantic reasons. She'd known it wouldn't be very nice – single men in blue-collar jobs back then lived in grim places – but she was shocked by the extent of its grimness and didn't want him to live there a second longer. With typical spontaneity, she said, 'Come and live with us.' And for some reason (probably that he was in love with her), he said OK – but on the condition that she sort herself out. Meaning the pills, because he wasn't an idiot.

My mother, having read Germaine Greer (and having a habit of telling people to mind their own business), told him it was no concern of his. He quite sensibly said it *would* be his concern if he was sharing a bedroom with a pill-crazed woman every night for the rest of his life. Put like that, she had to agree. And that was the start of her recovery.

It occurs to me that had Mr Holt not been so new to the town he might have had a good friend who might have warned him off. And this friend might have pointed out the awkward class difference and the problematic nature of the in-work relationship, especially with a junior colleague. They might have reminded him that he had been perfectly happy, for years and years, living alone in peace and quiet, listening to the wireless and reading political thrillers or books on history. And this hypothetical good friend might have told him that it would be utter madness to take on this drunken-divorcee-pillhead and her four children, however clever, pretty and knowledgeable about cricket she was.

But there was no sensible friend, sibling or parent around, thank God, and Mr Holt moved in. It was hard for him and for us. For the first month he still held the lease on the grim bedsit. He would go there for retreats and was barely able to force himself to come back to our madhouse. Our mother begged us to be on our absolute best behaviour and we begged her the same. And then, after a honeymoon period – during which we'd been as quiet and good as we could be, we went back to normal. Mr Holt couldn't cope with the chaos that was our norm and took to doing his paperwork on the way home from work, parked up in a field gate.

He couldn't believe we didn't have any routine, that we didn't clean our shoes on a certain day or go to bed at such and such time. There was no basic weekly agenda or timetable for shopping and laundry. He was shocked to see that my sister had made the bookcase into an aviary, by fixing chicken wire to the front, for her canaries, Pippy and Luke, and that our dog ate from a pudding basin.

We did all the things that kids do: we were noisy, we fought, made a mess and played with matches. And all the upsets and joys that happen in families happened. We broke things and he'd fix them. We upset the neighbours and he'd apologise for us. We got caught shop-lifting in the village and he'd shame us with his severe tellings-off, while our mother would lurk and worry and bite her nails and say he was too hard on us, and he would say she was deranged. And there were some awful, illegal and very bad things that I shan't go into.

There was the time the village policeman wanted to blame my brother for something, just to tick it off and have it solved, but Mr Holt fought it, like a lawyer in a book, until the policeman backed down. And the time I made a pie and wrote Mr Holt's first name in pastry letters on the top, and my mother said it was like something gruesome from Roald Dahl.

We were like any family and, though that doesn't sound all that exciting, it was, and still is, marvellous for us.

Mr Holt is a grandfather now, many times over, and though he still doesn't particularly enjoy a houseful of shrieking children (and you'd never catch him at a school play or a birthday party at the local Go Bananas) the kids love going to his allotment and nicking raspberries and carrots. They phone to ask him to run through the Cuban missile crisis for a school project, to talk about football or clarify something when Wikipedia isn't 100 per cent clear.

The narrator in my novel says thank you to Mr Holt, for giving up his savings, his privacy, his peace and quiet to move in with the fictional family.

Now I can thank him again, the real him, and tell him how proud I am of him and how grateful I am for his intelligence, humour and open-mindedness. It was a miracle we ever met him and ridiculous that he threw in his lot with us. Most extraordinary of all, though, is that we made a go of it. We grew to love each other and are still going strong forty years on.

Nina Stibbe comes from Leicester. Her stepdad appears in both her novels, *Man at the Helm* and *Paradise Lodge*.

MY DAD HAS BEEN FAMOUS LONGER THAN I'VE BEEN ALIVE

Tim Healy by Matthew Healy

My name is Matthew Timothy Healy. I was born naked in north London in April 1989. I am told it was quite warm – which has been the case for most of my birthdays. I am an adult now, semi-clothed. My father spent those early years of my life working between England and Australia – back-to-back winters that had deprived him of the sun for almost four years. He told me he remembers my birthday being a bright and memorable time, golden-hued. He currently lives in the house in which I spent most of my childhood. In some ways it exists as a shrine to what once was – our family and what has been achieved. It is a feeling that is comforting and unsettling in equal measure.

My dad, at five foot seven, a baby-turned-milkboy-turned-welder-turned-comic-turned-actor, was born in the early 1950s to parents Malcolm and Sadie, in Birtley, Newcastle upon

Tyne. He lived modestly up north, as a youngster and as a young man, with his brother, John, and their dog, Smartie (a dog that would later come to head-butt my dad in a moment of jestful play, resulting in him losing his bottom row of teeth. John once threw my dad over a wall, with the assumption that the drop on the other side was of equal height to that which he'd just hoisted his little brother over. It wasn't. He landed right on his head and has had to wear glasses ever since).

He would work between various factories during the day and at night he would pursue his dream of becoming a stand-up comedian. He is a very funny man, my dad, whose charm and passion is articulated through his comedy, and his face exudes a type of warmth that one would expect from a northern English comedic actor. He laughs like Muttley off *Wacky Races* and whistles inane tunes that have never been heard before, for good reason.

My dad has been famous longer than I've been alive. He was at the height of his fame just before I was born, during *Auf Wiedersehen, Pet*. My parents being famous was always part of my reality: there are photos of their wedding with a crowd of a thousand people outside looking in, which is what their life has been like. I know nothing different, and it bled into the way I saw myself. My dad was a rags-to-riches character, so as soon as he saw a stem of creativity in me, he knew the importance of nurturing it so that I gained a sense of self. Me being creative was always emotionally, financially endorsed by my dad.

'You're John Lennon,' he'd say, from the time I was six. He expected me to be a rock star, not in a superficial sense, but A Rock Star. Mark Knopfler from Dire Straits and Brian Johnson from AC/DC would occasionally come around to our house when I was growing up so it always seemed tangible.

Rock stars walked among us. Welders, too. Dad has that dichotomy between being a working-class manual worker and a bohemian actor. I remember watching a Michael Jackson video with some of his welder mates when I was a kid and them saying he was from another planet. I thought, Yeah. My planet.

My parents always taught me that you get the good with the bad. So, if you want to live in a nice house and have nice holidays, then maybe *Hello!* might have to come around your nice house or go on your nice holiday to take photos for their magazine. The *Daily Mail* and the *Mirror* went in a bit hard on my mum for a while, which was difficult for my dad as he's not from the tabloid world that comes with being behind the bar at the Rovers Return. He had to deal with a wife who was clinically depressed, being hounded by the tabloids. What does he do to look after his wife? We got through it. And there's stuff that people don't know. We found a lot of security in that, knowing that they only knew so much.

I thought about this a lot when my band was breaking. My mum is on *Loose Women*. That's not credible, that's not cool. My dad is a credible actor but he's well known too. Am I going to be perceived as an ITV boy-band thing? In the end I had to get over it. You can't judge musicians by what their parents do. It isn't going to work.

There are two things he always said to me, and always after a drink: 'Be who you want to be.' And 'It's in yer fucking bones, man!' He empowered me. He acted in awe of me. Not in a sycophantic way, but as if I didn't need his advice. If I had conviction, it would see me through – and that really rang true. Because I had a middle-class family I could get to twenty years old and still be working it out with the band.

27

I didn't go to university. I worked in a Chinese restaurant, which stressed my mum out. 'Is this band thing really going to become something?' she'd ask.

My dad never questioned it. 'Leave him alone, man, he's fucking John Lennon, man.' He believed in me unquestioningly from the moment I wrote a song called 'Robbers' when I was eighteen. He bought us our first van. He converted the garage into a rehearsal space. His overt passion for us is instilled in our band. When our album went platinum all of the band made sure he got a disc. He's the band's dad.

The character he plays in *Benidorm*, who rides around on roller-skates with a wig on and big boobs, is probably the one he sees the most of himself in. He told me he based it on a combination of Les Dawson and Tommy Cooper, which is my dad incarnate. If people ask me to describe my dad I say, 'Combine those two. That's him.' The slapstick he plays is quite like his real persona. He's a very, very good actor. It's not strange to see my dad put on a wig and be someone completely different. When it looks and feels like my dad but there's something else going on, that's when it throws me. It's the subtlety of my dad in the midst of a great performance that can really mess me up. If you're involved in the physique and the aura and the knowledge of who that person is, when the minutiae of it change it's quite alarming.

I steal a lot of lighters, which is something coincidentally I've stolen from my dad. We've stolen everybody's lighter we've ever come into contact with. Superficially, I think I'm more like my mother. I'm quite erratic. I'm passionate and emotionally driven, whereas my dad is more subdued about those things. I think what I've got from my dad is my fear of not being proud of myself. Those are the times I've seen him at his lowest, when he regrets something he could've done, mainly from a creative perspective. I've seen him cut himself up over things that I wouldn't have imagined he'd find that relevant or important. And then I find myself doing the same over a vocal take, or some small detail in a recording, and that's when I feel him inside me. That's when I know who I am.

Matthew Healy is the singer and guitarist with the 1975.

BUT I WAS SURPRISED THAT WE GRIEVE ALONE TOO

Mike Raphael by Amy Raphael

On the wall in my study I have a framed black-and-white photo of my dad, all black curly hair, discernibly Jewish nose, neatly trimmed beard and sixties polo neck, tenderly wiping my chubby cheeks. I am five, maybe six months old, so it must be the autumn of 1967. In an old black box there are more photos that connect us. A decade later, at my primary-school fair in west London, me wearing a Silver Jubilee badge, Dad standing nearby, his hair and beard bigger. In September 1977, in hospital, holding my newly born half-brother with a look of amusement on my face. Around the same time, me and Dad in a London park, the late-afternoon sun lighting up our curly hair.

One of the snapshots in the box of memories captures my mum in her twenties, patiently putting shoes on two-year-old me in yet another London park, her long, dark hair partly veiling her easy beauty. There are photos of old boyfriends and university friends; kittens that are long since gone. There are two photos of my dad. In one he looks uneasy, uptight. In the other his face is relaxed and he is smiling. The first was taken before he was diagnosed, very late in the day, with cancer. The second was taken after treatment. He is in remission. His curls have gone so he looks like a version of himself, but he is content.

There are no more photos. There was just a year between diagnosis and death. I was sixteen when he started treatment, seventeen when he died. He was forty-seven, the age I am now. It's thirty years since he was buried at Highgate Cemetery, close to his beloved Karl Marx. I still don't know if I really did stand alone by his grave, watching as the coffin was lowered and the soil scattered. All I know for sure is that I felt alone. I knew we die alone, but I was surprised that we grieve alone too.

While studying English at university, I recognised Hamlet's grief for his father. I saw it again in Mr. *Turner*, Mike Leigh's glorious film about J. M. W. Turner. Tim Spall, in the titular role, visits a young prostitute shortly after his beloved father's death. As he is sketching her, he suddenly, unexpectedly, howls with grief. It turns out that people don't always cry at funerals and that grief isn't always private. Sometimes a small act of kindness releases the grief – here, the prostitute, baffled by Turner's sexual disinterest in her, kindly asks if he would like a drink.

I, too, have howled, but internally, a silent tsunami of grief flooding my body. I see, sometimes, the effect on my face. A glimpse of disappointment, of loss, of why the fuck did Dad leave me? Time passes, but it doesn't numb the rawness or dull the ache. When I got to university, eight months after he'd died, I recklessly drank subsidised pints of snakebite and black. I dyed my big eighties hair black and danced to the Cult and the Sisters of Mercy. I kissed boys whose names I wasn't interested in. I cried in the dark when someone died in a film, hoping the credits would run till my cheeks were dry. None of my peers, away from home for the first time, most yet to experience loss, knew what to say to me.

The physical loss isn't quite the same when you haven't lived with a person since the age of four, but still I had questions to ask. I still *have* questions to ask. Yet I am lucky that we had time together. In London parks, camping in the countryside, eating sweets at the cinema.

These memories are, for me, spun from gold.

Before I turned ten, Dad took me to see *Monty Python and the Holy Grail* at the ICA. I didn't care much for the legend of King Arthur. I don't suppose I understood too many of the one-liners. But I sat next to my dad, laughing in the dark at the relentless slapstick, feeling like a proper grown-up.

A few years later, Bob Dylan at Earls Court on Saturday, 17 June 1978 (I still have the programme), his voice like sand and glue, bringing to life songs from my dad's vinyl collection: 'Mr Tambourine Man', 'Blowin' in the Wind', 'The Times They Are A-Changin'', 'You're a Big Girl Now'.

There are other, less specific memories. Swimming on a Saturday morning at the public pool in Swiss Cottage. Going to his squat on Camden Road (now, I think, a petrol station) and being tickled till I could no longer catch my breath. Eating fat handmade burgers at Camden Market years before either of us became vegetarian and decades before it became a tourist hell.

What else is left? My stepmother gave me some of Dad's jazz records. I hate jazz. She gave me his watch, but it broke as soon as I got to university. When he was ill, Dad spent time at the Bristol Cancer Help Centre, a holistic place where he got into carrot juice and art. He joked about turning orange and proudly showed me his drawings. Some displayed his political anger: his response to the miners' strike of 1984 to 1985 was to incorporate 'coal not dole' into as many images as possible. After he died, I hung one of his paintings in my bedroom. It was benign enough, abstract even, but somehow I could only see Dad's personal anger – why me? – and eventually I took it down.

My half-brother, who was seven when our dad died, says he doesn't remember him at all. I have to force my memory away from the dark (visiting Dad's flat after chemo and not being able to see him because he was too sick; going to the oncology ward alone to say goodbye) and towards the light. Whenever I open the black box, it is the second photo I now reach for. The photo where the curls have long gone but Dad is quietly smiling at the world. He is also, I like to think, smiling at me.

Amy Raphael is a biographer, journalist and writer. She lives in Hove with her daughter.

YOUR ELDEST CHILD GREETS YOU AND SENDS YOU LOVE

John Niven by John Niven

WOW. Has it really been twenty years since we last saw each other? Where did that go?

A minute ago, you were not long retired and I was just starting work in the music business. You turn around and – boof! – two whole decades have gone. Oh well, I guess time flies when you're dead and all. LOL!

Actually, that LOL will make zero sense to you. It means 'Laughing Out Loud'. It's very irritating and all the kids say it these days. It's from the Internet.

Oh, right, you missed the Internet too. Basically, we invented a way for us to have all the telly, all the movies, all your shopping, all your music, all your friends and all the entire historical knowledge of the world on your mobile phone. We mostly use it to settle arguments about football and arrange to meet people for drinks and sex.

Damn! I just realised you missed mobile phones too, didn't

you? When you popped off in 1993, they were still the size of a house brick attached to a briefcase and only bad guys in films used them, usually to tell the mayor they were about to blow up the city. Everyone has one now. Even wee kids. They're about the size of a pack of your beloved Regal.

Actually, the only person in Britain who didn't know that LOL meant Laughing Out Loud was David Cameron. He thought it meant Lots Of Love. He's prime minister, too, which gives you some idea of the kind of mess we're in.

I kid you not, Dad – the current government make Margaret Thatcher look like Florence Nightingale or the kindly old granddad from the Werther's Originals advert. Oh – bonus ball – Thatcher died!

I'll pause here to let you spend a few thousand years of your eternity laughing.

Done? Okay. Anyway, what else have you missed? Oh, Tiger. Right after you died, this black kid from America came along. Jesus, Dad, he hit the ball further than we used to go on holiday. He won everything – ten majors by the time he was thirty.

He's got fourteen now and it looked like he was going to beat Jack's record but then he kind of went crazy with the ladies.

It turned out he was having sex with everything in sight and his wife went tonto and battered him with a golf club and he hasn't won a major since. I still kind of like him, though Mum's not a fan.

Oh, Mum – she's well. It took her quite a while to get over you going so soon (as it did for all of us) but she's happy and healthy. She turned seventy a while ago. (I was going to say 'as you know' but remembering birthdays was never your greatest strength, was it?)

How about that? She's older now than you were when you

died. We had a wee party in Irvine. Everybody got drunk and had a grand time. You'd have liked it.

Not so grand down in Irvine now, though. The high street's pretty dead – lots of charity shops and pawnshops and the like. This was the other thing we didn't really figure out about the Internet – it ate everything.

They made a film of *The A-Team* recently and I thought, Oh, Dad would have liked to go and see that. (You and Gary loved *The A-Team* of a Saturday night, didn't you? I'd have been poncing about with a book, no doubt, mocking the pair of you. Sorry about that, about all the mocking.) But we'd have had a fair old drive – there are no cinemas in Irvine now. The bloody Internet ate all of them too.

Speaking of my brother Gary, I must now mention the saddest of news. He died four years ago in August. I'll give you another few thousand years of your eternity to come to terms with that. I'll just say this – he wasn't very well after you left and hopefully he's at peace now.

It occurs to me, describing all of this to you, that our lives since you've been gone have doubtless been like those of many families across the country for the last twenty years – a patchwork of tragedies and triumphs, of heartbreaks and joy. So, on to the joy now . . .

The clan continue to prosper. Your daughter Linda, my wee sister (God, there's another number that shocks you – she was nineteen when you died. You've now been gone longer than she even knew you for) had another baby, a wee girl called Aoife. It's an Irish name – you pronounce it Eefah.

You can imagine what Mum, Aunt Emily and Aunt Bell are making of this whole spelling vs pronunciation thing.

I think they're just going to call her Linda's New Baby for a while. This means you now have five grandchildren you never got to meet – Robin, Dale, Lila, Orlaith and Aoife.

They are all bright, happy children and you would be very proud. Robin, my boy, is seventeen. He's doing his Highers and is thinking about studying politics and law at university.

It often makes me think of Papa – your dad – being a blacksmith. From blacksmith to lawyer in four generations – that wouldn't be bad now, would it?

I wish you could have stuck around a little longer to see them all born but I guess, with the premature-death rates for Scottish men still being about the highest in Western Europe, I won't be the only man in his forties wishing his dad was still here to play with his grandchildren today.

I remember speaking at your funeral and saying something to the effect that, although you had died relatively young at sixty-eight, I wasn't too sad because I felt lucky to have known you at all. Boy, what did I know? I was only twenty-six and out of my tiny mind with grief.

Well, wherever you are, Dad (I still don't do the God thing), your eldest child greets you and sends you love.

Although it's not like today is particularly special because I think of you every day. Every. Single. Day.

You run through me unceasingly, like blood, like my own thoughts.

John Niven is a novelist and screenwriter.

'OI, JEMIMA, DO YOU WANT TO GO TO A PARTY?'

Ian Dury by Jemima Dury

I have a recurring image that my dad is Norman Stanley Fletcher in *Porridge*, and I'm Ingrid, his daughter. In my daydream we're sitting across from one another in Slade prison. I've got his full attention during visiting hours because Dad/Fletcher is trying, in spite of incarceration, to wangle a deal. 'Can you get me some gear?'

'Oh, Dad, what are you like? No, I can't and you shouldn't be asking. Oh, bloody hell, all right, then. I'll try.' What can I say? Fletcher, my pretend dad, is incorrigible.

Ian, my real dad, was incorrigible, too. It was almost his job description. How interesting that my subconscious cast him as Fletcher – a witty, unscrupulous petty criminal. And I'm Ingrid, his regular visitor, his invaluable confidante, and his long-suffering partner in crime. In an uncanny twist the Slade is an art school as well as a prison, so my subconscious gets top marks for irony. (Dad actually went to the Royal

College of Art but never mind.) I think of Dad and me as these two characters to amuse myself, but if anyone else asks me what our relationship was like then I think of the following anecdote. It's got all the right nuances and is not unlike the scene above.

On New Year's Eve in 1987, when I was eighteen going on nineteen, Dad asked me, 'Oi, Jemima-if-I-punch-you-in-the-ear'ole, do you want to go to a party?' I said yes straight away, thinking it might be rather glamorous and theatrical. I needed some excitement because I was having a bleak winter. For twelve months I'd been in Belgium, working as a dancer and experiencing much physical and mental endurance. It was a gruelling job with a theatre company and now I was back at home with my mum, no job, no prospects and no idea what to do with myself. It was time Ingrid paid Fletcher a visit: he certainly knew what to do with a creative void.

A party sounded like an adventure. I went to Dad's flat in the daytime so I could enjoy the preamble. I walked all the way from Chiswick to Hammersmith in my vintage dress, black tights, tons of goth make-up and big hair. He was on his own when I got there, which was great – not a girlfriend or ligger in sight. Good, I'd got some visiting hours to myself. That meant I would be on minder duty later when we went out. I loved minder duty. Usually, it was a job for Spider or Strangler but tonight Jemima was on the case. Being the minder involved toughness, strength and balance – toughness to stop him being hassled, strength to stop him falling over because the caliper he wore on his leg could make him unsteady, and balance to stop myself going over with him. I was very good at balance.

We sat through the afternoon watching TV and that was fine, the lull before the storm. Then, I was like Ingrid doing the chores while Fletch sat on his arse and gave it the verbal. After doing the washing-up and tidying, I made peanut butter and cheese sandwiches for dinner and we ate them followed by some grim chocolate desserts from Safeway. I thought, Hang on a minute, this isn't right, when Dad stayed put, in a committed way, to watch more TV. By eight o'clock it was starting to feel like a prison common room in there. He had two or three chairs in a semi-circle all facing a huge boxy television on an industrial trolley. It was like recreation time at Wormwood Scrubs.

So, I sat down again, too, in one of the expensive Practical Styling chairs, the pink one. One of the arms had fallen off and it was very upright so it was an uncomfortable expensive chair. More time passed and no sign of going out. He wasn't saying if he was having second thoughts but he wasn't giving off party vibes either. He wasn't getting dressed up or phoning a cab or reaching for the Chanel No. 5. (In two years' time it would be Body Shop Dewberry Oil.) By nine o'clock I was feeling depressed. I didn't want the evening to slip away. I knew it wasn't out of character for him to change his mind but it was New Year's Eve, for God's sake, and I was stuck indoors while people were out there discovering a new drug called Ecstasy and smooching to Chris de Burgh. Eventually we were slumped back as far as you can be in an upright chair and I was resigned to an evening of broadcast entertainment. One of the four channels was bound to come good.

He was never going to get out of that chair and I felt daft sitting there in brocade and black eyeliner. I've always hated the pressure of New Year when you're supposed to be some-where really exciting and meaningful at midnight otherwise you're sad and next year will be cast under a dark shadow. I gave in to it at some point, perhaps around ten o'clock and I must have thought, Oh, fuck it, that's it, then. The night had promised so much and delivered so little. So there we were, one daughter, who looked like a second-hand-shop turkey, and one forty-five-year-old rocker, who had gone off the boil, sitting in two very camp and uncomfortable chairs in a dilapidated flat staring at the TV. Bearing in mind that those were the days when you thought it was okay to stay in and watch Gary Glitter on New Year's Eve. So that was what we did.

After a long silence with very little conversation, he said, 'Have you got any marijuana?'

I played it cool. It didn't occur to me to think he was being blatantly opportunistic and outrageous asking me, his eighteen-year-old daughter, for drugs. Inside, I felt a glow of validation because he was treating me like a Level One grown-up. This was, without a shadow of a doubt, one of the proudest moments of my life so far with Dad. I'd earned my prison stripes. Believe me when I say the mention of drugs was inconsequential, because he smoked all the time. I knew it, and actually I preferred it to his drinking. But the fact that he'd decided to trust me with something so adult, well, that made me cool and in the gang. I'd love to know what he was thinking. Whatever it was, I conveniently came of age all of a sudden. It was like a desperate Fletcher had just asked Ingrid to smuggle a huge lump of dope into the clink inside a Dundee cake. This was the nod I'd been waiting for.

Now, I was not the pursuer or the purchaser of drugs as a rule. Fags, yes, I had smoked those since I was twelve, but anything else, well, I just wasn't very interested. How opportune for Dad, then, that on this night I did have a small piece of hash in the front of the dress I was wearing. The dress was silvery-blue and forties style (the sort you don't bother to wash), with two little pockets at the front near the waist, just the right size to hide and forget about a lump of dope. I'd had it for ages, since the summer, I think, and I was genuinely so nonplussed by it that I had forgotten it was there. It was only when Dad asked me the question that I remembered, and I was so keen to be a gang member that I felt extremely pleased with myself.

'Er, yeah, I have. Here you are.'

I swear that not one flicker of surprise or wonderment passed over his face when I handed over a bit of black stuff in cling-film. He laid a line of tobacco across two Rizlas and unwrapped my stash, then pulled out a Zippo and lit the hash. There was a fizzing sound and some black smoke, and whatever it was shot up his arm and disintegrated en route. It was only then that he looked up at me in surprise.

'That's a bit of asphalt, love.'

He didn't have to rub it in: I was mortified enough already as my fleeting kudos shot out of the door with the fumes of burning tarmac. He didn't rub it in because he'd probably been there too many times himself, in Notting Hill or Brixton, where spending twenty quid on a piece of rubber bin lid is not unheard of. Bollocks, I thought, as I remembered dropping the dope in the dark a few months before. I had obviously picked up part of the road and thought nothing of it. There isn't much more to say after this because he seemed to forget all about it and go back to smiling at the TV.

On paper, Dad's logic was completely immoral and suspect. He thought it was okay to lure me round to his flat on false pretences, get me to do lots of little jobs, build up my hopes and dash them, and then ask me for drugs. That was some interesting parenting. In reality, I barely remember any of that. What stands out for me is the fact that he accepted me as a regular experimenting teenager and didn't react when I screwed up the whole drugs thing. I know, I know, on paper that looks really bad but I'm so grateful he didn't bat an eyelid because then I didn't feel over-stupid and judged. I loved him for that. He never mentioned it again, not to me anyway, although once he got back to his cell he probably regaled Godber with stories of fizzing asphalt for hours. My dad's faulty logic provided me with many a tale to tell my fellow inmates, too. This episode concluded with Norman Stanley Fletcher and Ingrid settling back into their upright chairs and watching the Glitter Band play them into 1988.

Jemima Dury is looking after her dad's estate: music, art and writing. She lives in Hastings.

I PUNCHED HIM DOWN THE STAIRS

John Hamper by Billy Childish

I scarcely have a relationship with John, my father. He doesn't like to talk to me but I occasionally ring him up and the conversation will last for about thirty seconds. He has no interest in me, in how I do in the world and, more unusually, he isn't curious about his grandchildren. With our history you might think that I wouldn't talk to him or let him talk to his grandchildren, whereas I'm completely open to the idea. I think it's probably based upon his shame. My father is a complex, sociopathic narcissist. Not a bad guy, it's just the way God made him.

My father left home when I was seven but my mother didn't divorce him until my early twenties, when I beat him up because he was knocking my mother about. It was after he was released from prison for drug smuggling. He turned violent because she was finally planning to divorce him. I convinced her to do so because the creditors were coming and she was going to lose the house, and everything, and he was still with his girlfriend whom he'd done the drug smuggling with. He'd been violent to my mother in the past when my elder brother had been there and I always said if it happened when I was about I'd sort him out. So I punched him down the stairs.

It wasn't a long fight. I was twenty and he must have been getting on for fifty. He was fit for an alcoholic, but I was quite handy and my father is a bigger coward than me – and that is a big coward. The most alarming thing was that my father reverted to a five-year-old and started saying in a child's voice, 'I wouldn't hurt Mummy.'

About ten years later I made contact with John and we had a semblance of a conversation. I found out I had a younger half-brother. John said to me, 'Well, I've not been a good father, but what can I do about it now? Nothing.' He sees it as defining. Everything relates back to him. He can say sorry as long as it's about him saying sorry, but not about actually being sorry. It took me a long time to come to terms with it. What helped was that even as a youngster I never sought my father's approval. Rather than approval, I like to do what I like to do. In that respect I inherited something from my father because he is very individualistic. Where we differ is that I'm not good at lying. I also seek deep and meaningful relationships, and I can empathise. My father doesn't do empathy, and if he does, it's very, very private.

John's a very extreme character and entertaining for people who don't have him as a father. My brother can't have a relationship with him at all because it's too painful as he did seek approval. I call my father John and see him as a person. I love my father. I care about him to a degree but I have no expectation that I'll see him before he dies.

We were beaten a bit as children. My father's idea of discipline was to sneak behind us and smash our heads together if

I was arguing with my big brother. My brother was twice the size of me and to do that to a two-year-old and a six-year-old is extreme. I'm sure my father didn't invent this punishment and must have learnt it from his own father. I asked my auntie about how she and John were treated as children. Initially she said there was nothing unusual but I later learnt they were locked in a cellar, my father for two days at a time. Another thing I remember is my father issuing weird threats about the police coming to take me away when I was about three – just strange inappropriate conversations, really, and no love. I'd compensate by trying to get comfort from my mother but she's not particularly loving. Be warned: if you're bringing up children and you deprive them of love and kindness, you might end up with someone as crazy as me. (Actually, I've based my parenting skills on doing the exact opposite of what my parents did so it's not exactly a curse.)

After he left home I felt the absence of him, but I used to dread his return every three weeks to get his laundry done. So did my mother. This dread would settle on the house. He would go to his room and only communicate with us via my mother, conversations she only conducted in a whisper. She still only talks about him in a whisper. This has gone on my entire life and is hugely unpleasant.

My dad's an alcoholic and a womaniser. Both my older brother and myself followed in his footsteps. We believed that the way to get on in life was to have a constant supply of pornography, vast reserves of alcohol and a girl in every town. By the time I hit thirty, I realised that my constitution wasn't as strong as my father's and I had to give it up.

My father is a great pretender and quite delusional. Something to understand about John is that he comes across as a Michael Heseltine-type. He was a member of one of the oldest Masonic lodges in Britain, he was friends with some prominent members of the Tory Party, and prior to the drug smuggling, he was down to be a prospective Tory MP. You'd never guess his true background: a terraced house in Gillingham and a merchant seaman father. When he was arrested, I was the only one who had the guts to tell his working-class conservative parents. Everyone was scared they'd drop dead. I rang him when he was on remand at Reading jail. He came on the line and uttered one of my favourite lines of his: 'They're treating me like a bloody criminal!'

I have to say John is stranded in some kind of hell. He hasn't asked to be like this. As a son, it is a terrible loss for me. But what kind of loss is it for him? I can move past it: I've done several years of psychotherapy, I've done years of meditation, studied how to find a true meaning of worth and self. Whereas John is just stuck there. John would never have the courage, or opportunity, to do that. I'm lucky.

John turned eighty-one recently. I do ask myself how I'll feel when he dies. He's someone who's not been part of my life, but I'm sure I'll be upset and disappointed. Beyond that, what can I say? As a young man I thought my father was violent and that my mother and I were in danger of being murdered by him. I realise now that that was not the case. I wanted to kill him, but I'm very glad I didn't.

Billy Childish has released over 150 independent LPs, published five novels and more than forty-five collections of poetry, but his main job is painting. He is artist-in-residence at Chatham Historic Dockyard, the town where he also lives.

I NEEDED TO KNOW HOW TO ACT LIKE A DAUGHTER

Dave by Terri White

I always fantasised about being a daddy's girl. Watching my friends at junior school with their fathers – as they kissed, hugged and cadged lifts to the roller disco off them – I would study their easy interactions intensely, completely enthralled. It was important: I needed to know how to act like a daughter for when my dad came.

My mum and Dave collided in a rough pub one night: she was fifteen and furiously rebellious, he was twenty-one and promised danger. The day after she turned sixteen they were married – my granddad's offer of a horse, instead of a wedding, having been rejected. Within months she was pregnant with my brother. I popped out just shy of her nineteenth birthday.

What nobody disputes is that their marriage was a disaster. Before long my mum was painted with bruises and bearing broken bones. She later told me of the Christmas she couldn't see the turkey across the table, both eyes blackened and swollen completely shut under his fists.

His rage soon rained down on us all, and when I was two years old we left. After that, he was in our lives only very occasionally, even though he had access, before disappearing for months or years. He lived just six miles away with his new family, but I barely remember him.

What I do remember is this.

One of his (our) close relatives is getting married. It's also my eleventh birthday. I'm wearing a new dress from Tammy Girl and have spent a great deal of time blow-drying my perm. Me and my brother arrive at the local hotel just as everyone's tucking into their dinner. But there's been a misunderstanding. We aren't invited, only to the evening do, you see, and we certainly can't stay. We're led outside, into the street, and told to wait there for a few hours. It's freezing, my Tammy Girl frock offers little warmth, and as we sit on a bench by the roundabout and the sky turns dark, I start to cry. My defiantly dry-faced brother – who's already my eternal protector at just thirteen – comforts me.

Soon, contact petered out altogether. 'They know where I am if they want to see me,' he'd say, apparently. We did, and I for one didn't. Until I turned seventeen. Then I became suffocated by the need to find out who this man was. To find out who I was, really. And why I'd never been good enough to be his girl.

It was teatime on Boxing Day when I knocked on his door. 'Hello, duck,' he said, only moderately surprised. I went in, had a cup of tea, we made polite conversation, I left.

In the preceding years I'd watched *Surprise Surprise* avidly, imagining *our* reunion: the tears, the joy, the feeling of coming home. But there was no rush of love, no sense that I was inextricably his. Looking into his eyes – so much like mine – I knew he felt the same.

The next few years were punctuated by a series of painful stops and starts – each one resulting in rejection and confusion. It finally ended not unlike it began. I was nineteen and leaving for a summer abroad. It was also my birthday. He was coming round to say goodbye after he'd turned me away from his door. 'I'll be there at seven,' he promised. I sat by the window and waited, each set of passing headlights a fresh disappointment. As I started to cry, I remembered a similar scene – I was six or seven, we were supposed to be seeing Santa at the Co-op and I sat at the window for six hours, waiting. He didn't come then, and he wasn't going to come now. He would never come.

At 4 a.m., I closed the blinds and wiped my face. As I walked up the stairs I realised he wasn't a bad man; he just wasn't a dad. He wasn't my dad.

Terri White is a writer and the editor-in-chief of *Empire* magazine.

HIS TRUE CALLING WAS TO BE A RINGMASTER IN THE CIRCUS

Anthony John Martin by Chris Martin

My dad is a farmer's son from Devon. He grew up in an era where you couldn't really do what you wanted to do, you couldn't follow your true calling. It just wasn't allowed. It was the fifties, and his parents said, 'We think you should do this', and that was that. My dad's true calling was to be a ringmaster in the circus, but he missed the boat.

Now he comes on tour with us and that's the role he plays in life. He's a bit of an actor, and when he's backstage he makes everyone feel looked after. He's part of a team we have who go out into the crowd when we do big shows. Often we keep the first two or three rows empty. My dad goes to the back of the stadium and finds the kids wearing the T-shirts and says to them, 'Do you want to go and be right at the front?' He loves that. He loves meeting people, talking to them and connecting.

The frontman part of me comes from him. He sees the beauty and joy in everybody, no matter who they might seem when you first meet them. We've always got on well and he's always been very supportive, whether it was at sports days or when I was playing concerts. My parents sacrificed a lot to put us into a nice school and they really had to work their arses off. The main thing he gave me was the phrase 'Never give up.' As simple as it sounds: 'Never give up.' He'd often say it to me. I feel so grateful to my dad for that one simple thing. I use it all the time.

Chris Martin is the singer with Coldplay.

AS NEAR TO RESEMBLING A SEXY COMMUNIST SAINT AS SURELY EVER WALKED THIS EARTH

Bill Burchill by Julie Burchill

'Daddy's Girl'. It's such a horrible phrase, conjuring up so much a female can be, which is everything a hard-core feminist like myself despises. Some overgrown 'princess' (translation: a witless baby doll well on the way to being a useless Baby Jane, who needs her hand holding to open an envelope) 'practising' her 'female wiles' on some doting old dullard; in every way relatives can be revolting, this pair are.

My father – Bill Burchill, of Bristol – and I, on the other hand, fought like cat and dog from the moment my teenage hormones kicked in. Or, rather, I fought Fate like a cat in a bag on its way to a drowning, and my dad raised an eyebrow and took the dog *du jour* out for a walk whenever I started kicking off. I was, from an early age, convinced there was a plot to keep me away from my beloved London (the Crystal City, Oz, Eldorado, the home of the hallowed Underground map, which I hung above my bed and recited every night as if it would keep me safe) and condemn me to life in my slow-moving, easy-going hometown. I reacted to my redneck, blue-collar roots with vicious indignation – as one who was fighting for her very life, which in a way I was. The life I wanted, full of hard liquor and easy pickings, as opposed to accepting the fancifully named 'life' that had been prescribed for me as a working-class girl in the provincial England of the 1970s.

My father was a highly intelligent and extremely handsome man from a very poor family – his mother had to pawn her wedding ring every Monday and reclaim it every Friday as she had so many children and so little money, and a husband who loved beer more than he loved her – who, despite his God-given gifts, accepted his role in life not just with stoicism but with his own unique brand of modest arrogance: 'I'm BILL BURCHILL – what more do I need!' (He never said that, but you could tell he thought it.) He repeatedly refused promotion in the distillery where he worked, believing it to be an overseer's ruse to curtail his beloved trade-union activity – but he was a born leader of men, and he relished the fact. My favourite photo of him is not a family one, but a snap of him at some sort of work function: he is dressed smartly and has his shiny-shoed feet up on what is obviously a bigwig's desk. He smiles serenely at the camera while around him his mates, clutching pints, goggle and grin at his cheek, thrilled at his audacity.

If the class system had not had this nation in a stranglehold since the dawn of time, the ascent of millions of men like my father could have made this country a good deal greater than it was and certainly far better than the sad shell of a nation it is now. But staying put suited my old man. He saw the beauty in everything, especially his adored hometown of Bristol, whereas I saw only a backwater, which threatened to pull me under and kill me. So we were not, to say the least, similar – but I worshipped him nevertheless. I WAS a Daddy's Girl – that was my dark, shameful secret. It was the love that dared not speak its name, lest I decided all I wanted from life was A Man Just Like Him, and then I would be trapped, a prisoner of a pushchair before I could vote.

My father worked long, hard hours in the distillery, often on the night shift. My mother loved to sing – she was basically Mariah Carey behind a bacon slicer, with the good looks and temperament of the notorious diva but minus the actual voice. When it was time for my dad to be getting up she'd start in with popular songs featuring his name. Even at the age of thirteen, when I was immersing myself in the glorious filth of Bowie at his bending, blowing, buggering best, I would find myself singing pertinent phrases from the songs as I skulked around my bedroom dreaming of escape. 'I love him . . . because he's WONDERFUL/Because he's just my Bill' . . . 'My boy, Bill, he'll be tall and tough as a tree, will Bill!/Like a tree he'll grow with his head held high/And his feet planted firm on the ground/And you won't see nobody dare to try to boss or toss him around!' And the most annoying of all, to my ever-annoyed teenage ears, Laura Nyro's masterpiece 'Wedding Bell Blues': 'Bill, I love you so, I always will/ I look at you and see the passion eyes of May/Oh, but am I ever gonna see my wedding day – come on and marry me, BILL!'

'Oh, for fuck's sake!' I would whine. 'You're MARRIED, already!' Scrambling up the stairs, seeking sleazy sanctuary in the Velvet Underground, sickened by this flagrant display of marital pashing – and at the top of the stairs I would be greeted by my father's other greatest fan: Prince, an Alsatian dog, who saw it as his vocation in life to generally growl at, often snarl at and occasionally take a chunk out of anyone who dared approach my sleeping dad.

Mind you, you couldn't blame him. When they cast Sean Bean to play my old man in a BBC film I wrote about him and his dog, it was surely the first time that an actor (dreamy as Bean was) played a character more physically attractive than himself. But my dad treated the many women who fancied him (and even I, through my appalled hot-parent-hating eyes, could tell who they were) the way he treated the bosses who sought to promote him – with a sort of sarcastic incomprehension. He was only ever interested in my mother, and only ever fancied two famous women, so far as I know: the tennis player Billie Jean King and the actress Billie Whitelaw. My mother, in a moment of almost Wildean wit, once remarked to me as she was savagely ironing, 'Iss funny with yer dad, innit? People always says how modest 'ee is – but even the women 'ee fancies is called Bill!"

He was a factory worker, a car-park attendant and a man as near to resembling a sexy Communist saint as surely ever walked this earth. There wasn't a bad bone in that man's body, but I recall that he was as baffled by homosexuality as most men of his era. Whenever Lionel Blair or, indeed, any penis-owning prancer appeared on the TV screen, he would stare in sheer incomprehension for a moment, shake his head more in sorrow than in anger, call out, 'PRINCE/PATCH/BENITO!' (my father despised Fascism even more than he despised cats, but thought it would have been cruel and confusing to change our tail-wagging Il Duce's given name) and promptly leave the house with a creature you could rely upon not to plaster on the PanStik and do the fandango.

Which makes it all the more strange and beautiful that when I was ten years old, I came home from school one day and my father looked me straight in the face and said sternly, 'Bolshoi.'

I eyed him warily. Of course I knew what the Bolshoi was – I was a ballerina, tutored three evenings a week, a very likely candidate for the Royal Ballet School and had been since I was six and would be until my magnificent tits and towering height put me out of the running at the age of twelve. 'Bolshoi . . . BALLET?' I ventured.

My dad sighed heavily and attached the lead to the dog's collar. 'No, Bolshoi ruddy Bristol Rovers!'

I stared at him, stunned, as he and the dog walked away. 'We're going to the . . . Hippodrome? Next week? To see the Bolshoi?'

He looked back over his shoulder and winked at me. 'Box. Arm and a leg! Don't tell yer mother.'

As I recall, he read the *Morning Star*, then the Pink 'Un, then took out a pack of cards and played Solitaire as I sat beside him that night in the lushest box the Bristol Hippodrome had to offer, enraptured by the greatest Russian dancers of the second half of the twentieth century. When we got home, my mum was freaking. 'Bill, thee can't even see Lionel Blair on the telly for five minutes without taking the dog out! 'Ow did you manage to get through three hours of blokes with their bits out?'

He winked at me, kissed her on the cheek, put the dog's lead on and opened the door. 'Didn't LOOK, did I!' We heard his laughter as he walked into his street.

My father died of mesothelioma at the age of seventy. He had apparently caught it by working with asbestos as a teenager, building the early NHS hospitals – typical stoic show-off, he couldn't help himself from breaking the glad tidings to my mother and myself three years before he passed over thus: 'Doctor says I's a medical miracle. Iss been in there since I was sixteen! 'Ee said 'ee never seen nothin' like it – a body that tough.' Then he took the dog out as my mother and I uncharacteristically clung to each other, wailing. Nevertheless, I heard him laugh and speak to the dog sarcastically as they went into his street once more: 'Women!'

I moan a lot about nepotism but, as I write this, I realise that I, more than any of the half-witted, well-connected female columnists I bang on about, have benefited from it beyond all others. Because I was the only child of Bill Burchill, of Bristol. I was my father's daughter.

Julie Burchill is a writer.
She lives in Brighton.

DAVE WAS MORE POPULAR THAN I WAS

Dave Lynskey by Dorian Lynskey

A while ago, I interviewed the singer Robert Wyatt and came away thinking, Dave would have *loved* him. Wyatt is from the same generation as my dad and similar in some indefinable way, although Dave was neither a musical genius nor a committed Communist. Wyatt even smiled in recognition when I told him my name came from Dorian Hawkmoon, a character in Michael Moorcock's 1960s fantasy novels. (My mum had to put her foot down when Dave wanted my middle name to be Hawkmoon.)

I get this sensation a lot, this feeling that Dave is a phantom limb, and most keenly when I encounter art or artists. The comic-book exhibition at the British Library. The Guardians of the Galaxy. The vinyl revival. The Black Keys. So many times I wish he was there with me, so many things I know he would have enjoyed.

When I was young my mum used to ask him, with increasing

regularity and intensity, 'Why do you need all this *stuff?*' He was a pathological collector, bad with money, and loath to throw anything away, so my mum's house remains cluttered with dozens of boxes of books, comics, records and plastic models that she doesn't know what to do with. To her they're just baggage, but to him each one was an expression of creativity. Dave wasn't just a hoarder, he was a voracious enthusiast. Whenever I whined that I was bored, Dave used to say, 'Only boring people are bored,' because the world is so full of interesting things.

Dave (my choice; never 'Dad') was born in Brixton in 1946, a quintessential baby boomer. His family moved to Norfolk and he later regretted choosing to study at the University of East Anglia instead of moving away. Under pressure from his possessive mother to stay at home, he missed out on the liberations of campus life. He met my mum at teacher-training college in 1969 and took a series of teaching jobs, ending up at a school in the suburbs of south-east London, where I became 'Mr Lynskey's son'.

I get the impression that he didn't pull his weight when I was very small. Perhaps he struggled to connect with very small children and their endless quotidian needs and was waiting until I was old enough to share his obsessions – easier for me than for my sister. We started with model aeroplanes, spending hours together in the shed at the bottom of the garden. I still find the brand names exotically evocative: Aurora, Tamiya, Italeri, Revell. And the stern, unmusical German words printed on the tiny pots of paint: Olivgrun, Rotbraun, Dunkelgrau. Later came *Star Trek*, unnecessarily long war movies, the ghost stories of M. R. James, and Dave's old 1960s copies of *Mad* magazine, full of inscrutable in-jokes and bizarrely amusing parodies of films I'd never heard of.

When I was eleven, Dave came back from visiting his dying

father in hospital with a gift of *Uncanny X-Men #203* ('Phoenix Versus the Beyonder!'). That initiated an intense phase of father–son collecting, the two of us driving off to comic-book fairs in central London and the cluttered spare rooms of over-weight men wielding photocopied catalogues dense with almost unreadably small type, returning with armfuls of new acquisitions in protective Mylar bags. You can imagine my mum's delight.

When, for me, music eclipsed comic books, Dave was even more delighted. As a student, he had hung out at blues clubs and seen Pink Floyd headline at UEA. As a teacher in the seventies, he was obliged by law to like prog rock. He owned a harmonica that he had bought in a club from Rod Stewart, only to find minutes later that it had actually belonged to a furious Long John Baldry. Baldry gallantly let my dad keep the harmonica and stormed off to find thieving Rod. This anecdote might have been the first time I heard the word 'cunt'.

So, he was admirably patient when, for a whole year, I played nothing but Pet Shop Boys cassettes on the drive to school. He preferred Genesis. We brokered a compromise over Fleetwood Mac's *Tango in the Night*. When he died, I realised that his collection contained all the canonical classics but that he never played them to me because he was more excited about new bands that we could discover together: Nirvana, Nine Inch Nails, the Jesus and Mary Chain. He once turned up in his Ford Sierra after midnight to collect me and my friends from the Venue in New Cross without complaint. He just wanted to know if the band had been good.

At school I was known for having a 'cool' dad: a rare creature in the south London suburbs during the 1980s. The usual problem with becoming a teacher's son is that the other kids don't like your dad but, to be frank, Dave was more popular than I was. I think he had a rare genius for teaching: an unusual ability to treat children as equals without becoming a soft touch. He asked his pupils to write short stories based on the first page of an H. P. Lovecraft yarn and allowed dyslexic students to speak theirs into a Dictaphone before that was common practice. He used the school's first video camera to shoot a short film, which he edited to the sound of Holst's *The Planets*, and brought the hefty device home during the holidays so that I could make primitive stop-motion movies with my *Star Wars* figures. He organised school dances and began a quixotic unfinished project to create a school vinyl library of classic albums when everyone else had switched to cassette or CD. He loved to dance. He was the funniest person I knew.

Dave enjoyed anything I did that was creative or unorthodox. When I performed at a school concert with one of my spirited but incompetent covers bands, he was down the front with a video camera, admiring the audacity if not the results. After leaving school, I shaved my head into a mohawk with a curious, dangling fringe, a dreadful cut-and-shut of my own invention, and dyed it purple. Then I had to return for a prize-giving. Some of the teachers thought I was flicking a V-sign at the school (I suppose I was, a little bit) but Dave had my back.

This makes Dave sound more fun than he was. He could be surly, impatient and remote, spending his evenings painting model planes in the loft or plugged into his headphones at the far end of the living room. He could be bizarrely combative about things he wasn't that fussed about, guided by the principle that he needed to teach me how to argue. Given that he clashed with my mum on a daily basis, I already had a pretty good idea how arguments worked. I once had a blazing row with him about his voting Conservative in the 1992 election. After he died, my mum told me that he had in fact voted Green. I still can't work that one out.

I'm certain now that he suffered from depression. He was lonely because his university friends lived elsewhere and none of his colleagues or neighbours shared his interests. He seemed to find most people his own age disappointing, with their prosaic talk of jobs and schools and houses. I think his life would have been transformed by the Internet, where he could have found many fellow enthusiasts. Denied that, he bonded with the staff at record shops and comic-book stores and struck up some pen-pal friendships, including Isabel Monteiro from the band Drugstore. She kindly put us on the guest list when Drugstore supported the Jesus and Mary Chain at Shepherd's Bush Empire – the last concert I ever attended with Dave. My generation gave itself permission to stay young for longer, whereas he was considered eccentric for caring about new music past the age of thirty. Perhaps he was born too early.

Brought up in a post-war household, where emotions were as dangerous as unexploded bombs – best avoided – he was constitutionally incapable of discussing his fears and insecurities, so that was where all that *stuff* came in. As long as we were talking about Batman or *Quantum Leap* or Stephen King, we were fine and I was okay with that – probably too okay. There are too many gaps in my understanding of Dave, too many things I don't know because I never thought to find out. Like the chalk outline left on the ground after a dead body's been removed, all the details I have suggest the approximate shape of a life while drawing attention to its absence.

One strange thing about interviewing people for a living is that you realise you can ask someone you've just met in a hotel room how they felt about their parents, what their youthful ambitions were, whether or not they're happy, all the important things, while failing to put those questions to the people you love. I cringe when I remember being driven home from university in the holidays, jabbering away about all the thrilling new ideas I'd had about how the world worked, too full of being young and clever to coax Dave into talking about how he felt and then to actually *listen*. I take some consolation from my mum's revelation that he never discussed his feelings with her either – emotional reticence was baked in from childhood – but I could have at least tried.

The year after I left university, Dave fell ill. He had been diabetic since his teens, which often made him crabby. Now everything was going wrong at once. In quick succession, he had a heart bypass operation, a stroke, a diabetic blackout that caused him to crash the car, and kidney failure that required a dialysis machine. That was the blow that finally forced him to retire at fifty-two. I wasn't there. I had moved to London to start my career. I had fallen in love. I was busy doing important things like clubbing. I was your common-or-garden self-absorbed twentysomething. I thought he'd get better, mainly because I was too scared to consider the alternative. He wasn't old and I wasn't ready. He couldn't die yet. But he did.

What I remember from his final year is the stuff. The Black Sabbath CD I asked Ozzy Osbourne to autograph for him. Our last conversation at the hospital when I made him laugh by describing an Armstrong and Miller sketch about an inspir-ational teacher who stops caring the second the bell rings. His all-too-revealing obsession with Spiritualized's devastatingly sad 'Broken Heart', which I chose for his funeral in 2000 alongside his own choices, 'Spirit in the Sky' and 'A Whiter Shade of Pale'. Take away the books, the records, the TV shows, the movies, and what did we talk about? What did I know about him? Not enough.

So I don't tend to think about Dave when I'm with my wife or my daughters. I don't often consider what he was like as a father. I no longer have the recurring dream in which he's chatting away and I know that as soon as I break it to him that he's dead he will disappear. But, God, when I think about all the things he would have loved, all the shows he would have enjoyed by my side, all the interviews with musicians that would have given him a vicarious thrill, then he comes back to me.

Why did Dave need all that stuff? Because it was how he communicated best. And, in lieu of all the conversations we should have had, it's how I communicate with him still. Dave's passions were so numerous and varied that there are as many things that remind me of him as there are stars in the sky.

Dorian Lynskey is a journalist and author who lives in London.

THERE WAS NOTHING I COULD DO THAT WOULD SHOCK HIM

John Weller by Paul Weller

He was my best friend. As well as him being my dad, we had a long working relationship, from the age I wanted to get a band together when I was thirteen or fourteen. And we were lucky enough to continue that throughout my career, right up until he got ill towards the end. He was very supportive of me; one of those dads that whatever I was into he'd be right behind me. When I was into football he got a football team together, even though I was the worst player on the pitch. He was always up for whatever I was into. It was probably because he had such a lousy relationship with his own dad. That would always come out whenever we talked about being a father, how he didn't want to repeat what his dad had done. He'd always be encouraging. And then I got into music and he could see I was serious about it.

He was still working when I was getting The Jam together,

on the building site or on the cabs. He'd get a van, hustled off someone, and drive us to gigs. We'd have some gear but we also had to beg, borrow or steal other bits and he weighed in there too. Then he started getting us gigs. We'd go out in the week, the two of us, go round all the social clubs, working-men's clubs, Liberal clubs in Surrey and hustle gigs for the weekend. Then it started becoming a bit more serious and he became our manager, not so much reluctantly as nervously. I remember him saying to us around the time we got signed to Polydor, 'I'm not sure I can do this.' All of us said, 'Well, if you're not doing it then we're not.'

He learnt as he went along. He had no prior experience other than street smarts. But he was the manager when The Jam were signed. After the initial scramble when The Sex Pistols and The Clash got signed, all the labels went out to find their own punk band and we were coming in with the next tide. The A&R man from Polydor came and saw us at the Marquee and it all led on from that. We thought ourselves very lucky to have been signed. Six grand and we couldn't cash the cheques because none of us had a bank account. So my dad asked for it in cash. You can imagine how that went down.

I was eighteen coming up to nineteen around then, which was when I was meant to be rebelling, but there wasn't much to rebel against in my old man. He was a cool geezer. There was nothing I could do that would shock him or that he hadn't done himself – maybe drugs being an exception – and that could be a bit frustrating as a teen rebel. No cause.

But there were compensations. We always had a good relationship. If he was going to the working-men's club for a drink, I'd go along with him. We were always mates. It wasn't perfect: there were things that I did in my career that he wasn't always supportive of. Such as splitting The Jam up at our peak. That's probably top of the list. He thought that was mad. Like, *why* are you doing that? You're number one! Any manager would be like that, though. And even he came round to The Style Council after a while. But if we didn't see eye to eye then we'd have a tear-up and that would be that. Back to normal. You knew where you stood with him. He was brusque but charming with it. He was a bit of a bull in a china shop but you had to forgive him that.

Some of my happiest memories are after working on the building site with him when I was a kid, loading knocked-off gear into the back of the van that he'd borrowed. Also travelling back from gigs we'd played in clubs and pubs in London. After all the years of working-men's clubs in Surrey, it was just nice to see some youngsters again. Then coming down the A3 afterwards, being pissed in the back of the van, singing with him and the band. Those are some of the best memories.

It should have been difficult spending a lifetime together, but we had some of the best fun. The best memories nearly always involved booze, always shorts, never beer. He could drink a river dry of booze and still be bright and breezy in the morning. God knows how he did it, because he was only a little geezer. Nobody could ever work it out. Maybe he had hollow legs. I have so many memories of him reducing me to tears of laughter and some incredible scenes in my mind. Nearly always in bars. Hotel bars. Backstage bars. Airport bars. Lots of bars. I've got so many stories about him but none that anybody could print. So quick-witted that he got away with murder because of his charm. A Teddy Boy managing a rock band. Everyone just loved him.

I thought his passing was a blessing. He was really not in a good way the last four or five years – he was ill before that, but those last years were really sad to watch. It's a cliché but if he'd been an animal you'd have had him put down. This once proud, strong man looking like someone in constant turmoil was not good to see. You can never tell how you're going to feel with someone's passing. I wondered if I was going to fall apart, but I didn't because the person I knew had gone years before.

When I saw him dead in the hospital it was a beautiful April day, really sunny. The window was open and he looked at peace at last. I dealt with it okay because of that. I'm my father's son. He was strong and I have some of his strength of character. I also see the lineage of him and our forefathers in my kids. It's not so devastating when you can see that link passing down through the generations. I really believe that. He's still here in my kids, in me.

Paul Weller is a singer and songwriter. His previous groups include The Jam and The Style Council. He lives in London.

A DEAD MAGPIE PEEKED AROUND THE BEDROOM DOOR AND SAID 'HELLO'

Memories of Dad and animals by Rose Bretécher

Frogspawn – 1990

You came into Year One with a tank of frogspawn from our garden to show the boys and girls in my class. You said the funny clear stuff, which is like jelly, protects the little dots inside that will one day be frogs. You said they wouldn't survive without it. You said the adult frogs return to the place of their birth every year. The boys and girls in my class all looked into the tank and asked you a lot questions and I was proud because you were my dad.

Pigs – 1991

You took me and my brother to see the pigs on the twisty lane next to Hunkers Wood, where dormice and adders and skylarks lived. You sang your Pigs Lane song, which sounded a lot like your Heigh-Ho song and your Cow Lane song.

Puppy – 1992
You picked up the puppy and she fitted in your hand she was so tiny. When you put her in the basket by our kitchen door she cried and you touched her head and told her she was a good girl. You showed me how to stroke her without stretching her eyelids back.

Swallows – 1994
You took me for a walk on the Malvern Hills, which are as big as mountains, when the swallows were migrating in summer. Thousands and thousands, all the way to the Nile Valley, you said. You put me on your shoulders even though I was too big for that now, so I could try to reach them. You said I was at the top of the world.

Long-tailed tits – 1997
You wouldn't let me take them straight away, because you said the mother bird might come back, but when a cat started coming across the lawn you brought them inside. They were like two tiny balls of cotton wool and their eyes were like tiny black beads. They were shivering and I wanted to hold them to keep them warm but you wouldn't let me. You said I could talk to them while you went to find worms and caterpillars, and I did, but they died. I said it wasn't fair and you said Nature isn't fair, and I stomped away from you.

Tadpoles – 1998
The tadpoles were nearly adults, so you said I ought to see them while I had the chance. They still couldn't live independently outside the pond, you said, but they were coming

closer to the surface because they were starting to breathe in a different way. I groaned and walked off. You'd shown me them a trillion times before.

Woodlice – 2000

I was trying to make a good impression because it was the first time my sister's boyfriend had been round for dinner. You came in from the garage and demanded to know who'd been spitting on the woodlice in the back loo.

Pheasant – 2002

I was bored on a Saturday afternoon when you came home with a dead pheasant. You'd accidentally run it over and thought it'd be fun to show me how to pluck and gut it. It was totally gross. You held up the kidneys to your ears like earrings. I told you I had better things to do and went into town.

Dog – 2004

I was away at uni when the dog got put to sleep, but you told me about it on the phone. While it was happening you touched her head and told her she was good girl.

Magpie – 2011

I was up from London with my new boyfriend. It was the first time you'd met him. In the morning, while we were still in bed, a dead magpie peeked around the bedroom door and said, 'Hello,' then did a little dance to a tune that sounded a lot like your Pigs Lane song. You'd found the bird in the garden and thought it too beautiful not to show us. My boyfriend took a photo. I love that photo more than words can say.

Frogs – 2015

I called you on my way home from work, tired and clammy from the Central Line. When you answered you were breathless because you'd rushed up from the garden, where you'd been showing your granddaughter the new frogs under the beech ferns by the pond. I was jealous. You once said that adult frogs return to the place of their birth every year. So often, in the big city, I want to return to mine.

Rose Bretécher is an author and writer living in London. Her first book, *Pure*, was published in 2015.

HE PAID FOR EVERYTHING WITH A CREDIT CARD, ALWAYS EMBOSSED WITH A DIFFERENT NAME

Mohammed El Tahtawy by Yasmin Lajoie

When they first met he told her that he was a doctor. She found out the truth, that he'd never had a proper job, a few months later but married him anyway. He was a charmer, my old man. That's what Mum always said.

They divorced before I can remember and, following a messy abduction attempt, my mother was granted full custody. When he got out of prison, though, he repeatedly took her to court, exhausting legal aid and pushing for more and more of me and my brother until he had regular unsupervised visits. A lot of the time he never came and left us waiting for hours. His excuses were incredible: there was a fire, he broke his arm, he had malaria.

When he did show up, he bought us stuff, I think maybe

because he didn't know how else to love. Video games, trainers, mobile phones. He paid for everything with a credit card, always embossed with a different name. I remember once, in Toys R Us, he was Omar Sharif.

My younger brother got more than me because he was a boy. More pocket money, more presents, more praise, more *everything*. I was told to be pretty and shut up because men didn't like smart girls, and I was too young and inarticulate to argue. Feminism was left to gestate inside me – an embryo of outrage and indignation.

Quite often he was with his other family in faraway places (Cairo! Beijing!) but he would always come back into our lives, popping up every year or so with his presents and his lies and his indefinite leave to remain.

When I was thirteen I decided I didn't want to see him any more. It was something small that broke me – I can't even remember what he said or did. But that was it: I told him that I had run out of hurt. I changed my name. I was stubborn. I wished that he would die.

Then, suddenly, two years later, he did die. He was on a night bus coming back from a club when a drunken teenager grabbed the wheel and steered it into a railway bridge. There were journalists calling around our house, a five-and-a-half-year sentence for manslaughter, a girlfriend we didn't know about. All the little things that follow a death, all the paperwork and the lawyers. The compensation, his repatriation, my special consideration. The women at his funeral wailing until they coughed up blood.

We went through his belongings. My brother took his watch, his passport, life remnants. I found a letter from WaterAid, addressed to his real name. Thank you for your kind donation, it said. At fifteen years old my black-and-white world instantly became muddy, contaminated. He wasn't evil. He was like me. Grey. Complicated.

You can't eject people from your life without expecting any fallout. My dad is there in the parts of me that I can't reconcile with the person I want to be. My mania and depression, how I'm late for everything, the intensity of my thoughts, my selfishness. Sometimes I lie so convincingly that it terrifies me. That's him. Sometimes I get drunk and break things. That's him too.

Before he died, I imagined that one day he would apologise, I would forgive him and it would all be okay; that there would be some kind of redemption. I still kind of hope that this is a long con, one of his stupid excuses for not showing up. I still look out for him every time I'm at the airport: the man with many names who travelled the world and gave to charity, who was charming and clever and complex. I half expect to see him picking up a carton of Marlboro in duty-free.

Yasmin Lajoie lives in London and works in the music industry.

'ROY, THIS IS FIONA AND SHE IS IN LOVE WITH YOU'

Roy Castle by Ben Castle

I didn't realise that growing up with my dad was any different from growing up with anybody else's dad at the time. He was the only dad I had. I knew he was on telly a lot, but I didn't always watch it. I just knew that was his job. I watched *Record Breakers* and I often enjoyed it, but I was always more keen on whatever was on the other side. Once I was in his dressing room at the Palladium when he was in *Singin' in the Rain* and I was moody because *T. J. Hooker* was about to come on telly and I couldn't watch it.

'But, Dad, it's my favourite TV programme!'

I looked at his face and I knew I should've said it was my second-favourite TV programme. It was a terrible awkward moment I couldn't come back from.

He was not a stern dad. If ever he had to get cross with us, he'd employ my mum to do it. I remember once when my sister had been naughty my mum said to her, 'Ooh, you wait until your dad gets home.'

When he got home, Mum told him to sort my sister out. So he went up to her room and said, 'Look, Mum's told me to get cross with you, so if she asks, I have, all right?'

There was always so much music in the house. I was into a lot of rock from a very young age. I got completely hooked into Deep Purple for some reason from the age of nine. It was 1982 so it wasn't exactly boom time for them. They'd split up, for a start. But, nevertheless, through my cousins I got hopelessly addicted to Deep Purple and all the other heavy bands around then. It wasn't particularly my dad's cup of tea but he encouraged me to get into it, to enjoy any kind of music. He lured me into jazz eventually and was always playing Frank Sinatra. He also played a lot of Clifford Brown, who was a fantastic trumpet player, so I got into all that as well. I loved the rock, but I loved the jazz, too, thanks to him.

Despite my dad having a long career in the spotlight, he wasn't particularly showbiz away from his work. The most showbiz thing that happened to my family was my parents being introduced by Eric Morecambe. My mother used to sing and dance in West End musicals. She'd done pantomime with Morecambe and Wise a few times and was good friends with them. She'd seen my dad on telly – he had his own series, which Morecambe and Wise had been on, and she had taken a shine to him. So she said to Eric once that if he ever got the chance could he introduce her to Roy Castle. The next time my dad did a show with them, Eric Morecambe brought my mum into the dressing room and said, 'Roy, this is Fiona and she is in love with you,' and then he left. And that was it, there was never anyone else.

I didn't really know who Eric Morecambe was, growing up, other than the man who would have our whole family crying with laughter when we went round to his house for lunch. Eric died when I was ten, so the talent to have everyone from a nine-year-old boy to adults in their fifties in stitches with an off-the-cuff comment was a kind of true genius. That was another privilege of having Roy Castle as your dad: lunch with his best friends, Eric Morecambe and Harry Secombe.

My dad never talked about his career at home. It was only after he died that I discovered the albums he had made. And he never mentioned the films, such as *Carry On Up the Khyber*. I only found out about it when I was staying at a friend's house. We went to bed, and then his mum woke us up, saying, 'Quick, come and watch this!' I remember the brilliant feeling of me and this other family laughing hysterically at my dad and Sid James being covered in plaster as a ceiling fell in on them on television. Having said that, all my friends wanted to meet my dad because *Record Breakers* was one of the shows that everyone watched. It was a strange thing when he'd pick me up from school and everyone was asking for his autograph.

He broke a lot of world records on *Record Breakers* and when you start to list them it seems utterly bizarre that one man, my dad, could have done it all. They're so random. When it started they got him to break a few just to get it going. He broke one for playing the most musical instruments at once and also for playing the most taps in a second, which is twenty-four. Then, because he was the face of the programme, if there was a generic record to set he'd attempt it. He was the head helmet of the most white helmets standing on each other as a triangle on top of a motorbike; paragliding under the most London bridges. That kind of caper. He did the death slide from the top of Blackpool Tower, despite being petrified of heights. He also did the wing walk over the English Channel. Many years later, I was stranded on a plane in the snow next to this lady who started telling me about all the times she'd been stuck in airports. She told me about the one time she'd been stuck in Cairo airport because bloody Roy Castle was wing-walking in the wrong airspace and nobody could take off. She said she'd never loathed a man more than Roy Castle that day. I left my ticket in my seat for her to see my surname. Hopefully she googled me.

My dad's advice to me was to find out what I thought I was good at and stick to it. He always felt that, because he did so much, nobody knew what he was best at. Different generations remember him differently. For some he was a comedian, for others he was an actor or a jazz musician, and for my generation he was a children's TV presenter. But he felt his main thing was singing. That was his passion. Frank Sinatra gave him an album deal with Reprise. I found the telegram from Sinatra welcoming him to Reprise when Mum was moving house. Frank said he would be a global superstar, and the album is absolutely brilliant. But it was the early sixties and Elvis and the Beatles were about to change music. Big-band crooners didn't stand a chance.

From the outside, he was an enormous, multi-talented success, but when you're in it you don't necessarily feel that. There's always more you could be doing. Sinatra had said they'd make movies together, and when you've had that suggested to you then you wonder if you've fulfilled your potential. But, in Dad's words, maybe if he'd done all that he might not have had the family life we enjoyed.

I remember his diagnosis. My parents had been away in Australia on holiday over New Year. When they came back he had these terrible migraines that he'd never had before. All through the night he'd be pacing up and down along the corridor because he couldn't settle. He went and got tested for all sorts of things but they couldn't work out what it was, so they put him on various different diets. Eventually they found out he had a shadow on his lung and it was inoperable cancer. It was chemo or radiation only. I had a band rehearsal in the garage when he was at the doctor's and I came up to the house to find out. I knew from their faces the news wasn't good. When the words came out of his mouth the world caved in.

My dad was a Yorkshireman who grew up in a one-up-one-down house, sharing a bedroom with his parents until he was fifteen. He was a stoic man. He wasn't someone who was prone to showing too much emotion. So to see him cry was a very unusual thing. It was huge. He was only given six months, although he managed to live for two and a half years.

Those two and a half years were exhausting, emotionally. A series of hopeful periods and setbacks. We never courted any publicity throughout but it had obviously touched people's hearts because he was constantly in the newspapers. That was an embarrassment to him.

There was a point when the doctors were happy that it had gone away. That was just amazing. The all-clear: what a moment. My dad used to drum on the table a lot, though. He did a show about George Gershwin and he knew that Gershwin died of a brain tumour. Gershwin had noticed it because his left hand wasn't as fast as his right hand when playing the runs. We had some guests round for dinner and my dad finished drumming on the table and said, 'Tomorrow I'm going to go to the doctor and they're going to tell me I have a brain tumour.' He was right. He got very ill.

That was such a huge blow, although maybe not quite as hard as it might have been had we not still been wearing our armour from the first diagnosis. To misquote Alan Partridge: needless to say, we laughed through it all. In our family we've always laughed, even in the darkest moments. Dad was so positive. He was either on, out campaigning, or he'd be collapsed. Sometimes he needed to be wheeled around. But as soon as he was on stage or on camera he was bright as a button. My dad used to call that Dr Footlights.

Towards the end he went round the country on a train campaigning about lung cancer and increasing awareness of passive smoking, which is what the doctors had put it down to. It was just the final few weeks when he wasn't well enough to leave the house and gave that up. He was unstoppable otherwise. It was exhausting to watch.

The older I get, the more I understand him. The more I relate to him. I would love to ask him all kinds of questions about what he did because I feel like we are very similar in some ways. People say how alike we are, and that's a bit embarrassing, but I do feel a real connection with him now. I used to do gigs with him, from the age of nine. I'd play clarinet. He'd written this thing which was a comedy routine with music. I'd play a piece of music, he'd accompany me on the piano, and then we'd get faster and faster until he waved a white flag. It was very generous of him. That was the moment that I thought, I love this. I very rarely get nervous now on stage because of that apprenticeship.

Looking back, it seems like an idyllic childhood. At the time I didn't realise it, but talking to friends I now see how lucky I was. I'm so incredibly grateful. I have one brother and two sisters and we're still a very close family. We still go round to my mum's for Sunday lunch. We all just wish he was there too.

Ben Castle is a musician and lives in London.

HERE I WAS, THE APPRENTICE TO THE MASTER

Wally Downes by Wally Downes Jr

Trying to live up to your dad's expectations is one thing. Trying to do it when he's your boss is another. Attempting both while in the midst of a relationship hiatus (blazing row) is a Shakespearean tragedy wrapped up in a Monty Python sketch.

I was given an apprenticeship at Brentford Football Club after finishing school, despite being an inch off dwarfism and about as quick as treacle. It was like nothing you could ever imagine: an actual paradise. Living rent-free indoors, getting fed and clothed by the club and having a Professional Football Association card that ensured we could get into the local nightclub three times a week as VIPs – I'd not long packed up my paper round.

The only thorn in my side was that my old man was the boss. He wasn't at the start, oh, no. At the start it was easy. I would trundle along with my pals, giggling from 8 a.m. until 5 p.m. while cleaning boots, getting beat up, larking about, lifting weights, laughing and playing football. But a few months in, Dad got the job as manager.

Him and Mum had split up the year before so I was the man of his vacated house. I was having sex at least once a week and earning forty pounds just as regularly and I had nine average GCSEs to fall back on whenever I saw fit. I thought I would demonstrate my new-found worldliness and machismo as often as possible.

I can't remember what we rowed about initially. A feud of any kind is a doddle to bring on, isn't it? You ignore calls and emails, you maybe stop going to a certain pub, you de-friend someone on Myspace. Yet here I was, the apprentice to the master, and we weren't talking. I must have walked past him fifty times a day, made him cups of tea and cleaned his boots, all with a solemn vow of silence. God knows what it must have looked like to the other boys around me – there was enough to mock me for without a soap opera unfolding before them.

As a stout dwarf I was determined to lift heavy weights and would get in early to bench-press myself senseless. One morning I was casually trying to lift my own body weight without any assistance. Aiming for five reps, I got three in and my world started to cave in: arms buckled, veins bulged, and slowly I could see a pair of flip-flopped socks and WD-initialled shorts meandering towards my stricken body.

And there he stood, hovering over me like the Lord Almighty, wafting above my spasming body as the bastard weights bar hung over me like the sword of Damocles. Fuelled by his presence I somehow knocked the last reps out and he toddled off, muttering something ever-so-casually under his breath that was the perfect blend of praise and condescension, like, 'You're quite good at that.' I was so glad I got it up – and pissed off I was still the little div so eager to impress the boss, I mean Dad, I mean boss . . . *Him.*

I look back and cringe. It was the height of embarrassment. Every morning the boss would stroll in and greet the dozen herberts sat in the dressing room discussing their latest conquest, and I would maintain a stoic silence – a real challenge given the level of lairy obnoxiousness I was operating at the rest of the time.

One Christmas he cornered me in the tea room at Griffin Park, Brentford's ground, and lovingly presented me with an envelope filled with vouchers for the latest trendy shoe shop in Chiswick – clearly unaware that at the start of my second year in football the pay was bumped up to a lofty forty-five pounds and I was walking around in the grooviest size sixes in town. I politely refused. In a *faux*-vicious attack he threw the envelope in my direction but, in the unpredictable way only an envelope can fly, it immediately darted to the right, about four foot in front of me, smashed into the wall and slowly slid down. I stifled a giggle at the spectacle but he was having none of it. I'm sure he wanted to laugh, really.

I'd still get horrible pangs of love and loyalty especially when fans at Brentford would harangue him from the sidelines. I was desperate for him to do well and hated hearing chants of 'Downes Out'. But I was all bravado and felt I had the upper hand. I was pushing heavier weights and getting more hirsute by the day, and my recent acquisition of a National Identity Card meant I could venture from Kingston and sow my oats as far away as Hammersmith and Putney.

Of course, it all came to a juddering and almighty collapse. I was injured at the time but I remember seeing a load of the boys walking in from their latest session looking grey. All but two of the gang had been released there and then by the youth team manager and two of my best pals were among them. Seeing those fellas cry in the dressing room was horrible and I completely melted.

I knew it was all over and the idyllic bubble we lived in had burst. I walked out of the Tolworth base devastated because my friends had been let go, and I was never going to return as their talent far exceeded mine. Just as I thought my sob-ridden dash to the 281 bus stop was a clear run, Dad caught up with me, and the bolshy little twerp – all Jean Paul Gaultier aftershave and John, Paul, George and Ringo attitude – reverted to embryo.

All the iron I'd been pumping couldn't pull me out of his bear hug, and all the Dax hair wax I had caked into my locks did not deter him from nuzzling into the pathetic-looking creature he had spawned. Through a torrent of tears and snot I howled how unfair it was that my pals had been axed and the cold manner in which it had happened, paying no attention to the stony wall of silence I had erected in front of my dad for so long. I let it all out, he didn't say much, and that was that.

I toddled off with my wounded mates to get drunk, and the next day Dad had work for the three of us lined up from the minute we sobered up and pulled ourselves together. The phone calls got answered, I taught him how to use email and we started to frequent the same pubs.

It's all been plain sailing since. We fuck up and forgive and repeat the well-trodden route over and over now. Landmark moments, like successful driving tests and graduations on my part, and what seems like a relentless stream of Premier League promotions on his behalf have been joyfully shared with raucous laughter instead of begrudging hush.

Perhaps the memory of that deafening silence is what prevents a recurrence. We're not exactly quiet, Dad and me. And while the scent of tobacco and Brylcreem reminds me of my granddad, it's the old man's wall of sound I associate with him most. And that prolonged self-enforced silence might be why there's rarely a quiet moment between us now and why I dread the day when there'll be no more phone calls at silly o'clock in the morning, telling me he's wiped everything off his iPad and I need to rush round.

Wally Downes Jr comes from a family of esteemed sportsmen but – after a near-death experience with pyloric stenosis – he shunned athletic glory for sports reporting.

HE WOULD BE QUIETLY IN THE BACKGROUND

the only wog in the world by Tjinder Singh

my father was in many ways there, but not there at all. not that he was a rogue like a lot of men i can remember growing up, but like Peter Sellers in the Party he would be quietly in the background, trying to keep away from trouble when he was outside the house, and like Enid Blyton's Uncle Quentin he secluded himself when he was at home.

we had a very decent upbringing in Enoch Powell's Wolverhampton, and my father, the youngest man at that time to ever make it to the grade of Headmaster in the Punjab, decided to go to England and bat for the India First XI. metaphorically that is. as he was a man of learning and few words it was really when he passed away and left the crease that I started thinking more of him, of him more, and probably like most people who have had a child or two, or go through a few perilous times or twenty, these thoughts start to cement over time.

massaged into his conversation were all of life's stories retold in no particular order, and it's that lack of order and piecing together that makes it that much more compelling to hear again and again, until even the most un-attentive bastard commits. very similar to listening to the best music albums, you complete dimwit.

he never swore. he was never dishonest. he never laughed much but when he did the whole of the Black Country laughed with him.

as his teacher re-training never quite got him back to the standard he had achieved in India, he lived a life in the shadow of what life should have been, and was rather disappointed with his lot as the overs passed away. yet in his kids' eyes, in which he was too consumed to find any solace, he was the only wog in the world.

there were a few summers when he would come and watch us play cricket, or more precisely inspect a clump of mound to see what makes it mound. nowadays i join him there sometimes, just shy of the boundary, walking with our arms behind our backs, and holes in our conversation. i hope that ball is not coming our way.

Tjinder Singh is the singer, songwriter and producer with the group Cornershop.

HIS IMMINENT DEMISE WAS PROPHESIED WHEN HE WAS ONLY 35

David Michael Griffiths
by Joanna Kavenna

My father, David Michael Griffiths, was a bold and brave man who refused to listen to prevailing advice from doctors. He really confounded medical experts the length and breadth of the nation. His imminent demise was prophesied when he was only thirty-five. The edict was reiterated, with greater force, when he was forty. Thereafter, his life was tenuously sustained in increments – three more years, five more years. At fifty, he was told it was absolutely certain he wouldn't live to sixty. With bloody-minded determination, he continued. His Houdini evasions of adamantine medical fact became so daring and unlikely that when he died at the age of sixty-nine, in 2014, it was even a shock. He had fended off so many crises in the past, one crisis, then another. It was only when everything went wrong, when his organs all failed at the same time, that he finally surrendered.

My father was born in Reading, on the fifth day of the fifth month, 1945. When the war ended, his parents moved to north London. He was a brilliant child, much loved and applauded – the lone prospect of a rambling Welsh family that had largely forgotten to produce heirs. His grandfather, James Griffiths, was born in a hovel on the Pembrokeshire coast – on stormy nights the waves broke across the hearth. At the age of twelve, James was expelled from school for putting gunpowder in his teacher's pipe; after that he ran away to sea, survived two shipwrecks off the Cape of Good Hope, and rose to the rank of captain. Later, this formidable seafaring maniac went back to Wales, and became a fervent campaigner against social injustice and poverty and, eventually, a Labour mayor of Cardiff. My father's uncles were sailors too, and served on naval convoys during the Second World War. This heritage, and my father's early life in the bomb-damaged city of London, affected him greatly and determined his ensuing course. He was obsessed all his life with the history of the Second World War. He eventually became an expert on avionics and radar technology. He made his way by sheer hard work and cleverness; he was the first in his family to get the chance to go to university, and – to the amazement of his parents – won a scholarship to Cambridge.

Later, he met my mother, and they married in a jovial, informal wedding – everyone wearing preposterous hats and smiles. My father assumed the guises of the family man: he committed himself to cataclysmic enterprises in DIY, likewise sundry mini-tragedies of gardening; he spray-painted our car avant-garde two-tone shades and produced ambitious cuisine, which his family devoured like happy philistines. He protested mildly when his daughter played the piano, guitar and, worst of all, the violin (badly), when he wanted to sit quietly and leaf through his stacks and stacks of books. He was calm, kind and gentle, and such words recurred in every eulogy after his death – commendation after commendation – from those who said he'd helped them in so many unobtrusive ways.

When I was a child, he seemed a tall, unknowable figure, a book in his hand, exiled into our garage and leaning against the freezer. If I wanted to consult him on matters of global history or military campaigns of the recent past or the writings of D. H. Lawrence, which he discussed for hours – and then later revealed, to my consternation, that he had never read – I would knock on the garage door and find my father immersed in one more book, always oblivious to the carnage around him. He was like a chain-smoking oracle with eccentric taste in interior design. He knew so many facts, so many histories. His memory was formidable.

I used to ask him questions about anything and he always answered them. It was a game, all the time I knew him. What would happen if the earth stopped spinning? Why is the sky black at night? My father contemplated the mythical rites of moon worship, pagan cults, forgotten shrines and the druids of England and Wales. He relayed historical events in considered detail, mused liberally on the Ancient Sumerians, the philosophical Greeks, the symbolic nature of Clock Time – and so on . . . He never did anything with this knowledge: he simply didn't have the urge to churn it into books or convey it to the world. He didn't much care about those sorts of wider plaudits.

He was a great and unpredictable traveller, who roamed widely, across the Americas, Scandinavia, Asia and the Middle East. Most of all, he loved the sea. He spent family holidays sailing boats, in the Lake District, on the Norfolk Broads. He taught himself to sail – mostly from books – and he also liked a drink; this combination of factors meant that occasionally he did not exactly sail his boats but more precisely wrecked them against inconvenient land masses that had decided to get in the way. All my earliest memories of my father are related to boats and sailing – his craggy handsome face, silhouetted against a hazy dusk, the first stars rising. Smoke drifting from the inevitable cigarette, as he stares upwards, checking the direction of the wind. The gurgling sound of the boat, moving through water. My father was brought up in landlocked north London, but he cultivated inherited passions and, when I was four, moved our family to Suffolk. A beautiful stark coast of flat mud plains, silver estuaries, seabirds fluttering onto reed beds, lonely windmills. My father spread tidal charts across our kitchen table, along with, to my mother's unmitigated delight, an obsolete GPS device, a few emergency flares and a broken outboard motor.

He imbued me with his love of the ocean, as well as a propensity for reading and hoarding books. In his small three-bedroomed house, he amassed an incongruously extensive library. He possessed in general more model trains and aeroplanes and model things and things in general than anyone I have ever met. He was shy and strong-willed at the same time; he specialised in witty, subversive asides, so you perceived that he thought deeply and distinctively about the world. He once told me that he was forced out of a long barrow, at West Kennet, by the ghosts of the departed. He also believed he could move through houses he had once inhabited, actually return to them, in some metaphysical or imaginary sense. He retired to Machynlleth in mid-Wales, or tried to, though his health was poor by then. There he had a small slate house with a view of the River Dyfi glittering beyond the fields, seabirds reeling across the sky. To him, proximity to water, to any ocean, was bliss.

My father was so ill, and so evidently refusing to be ill, for so many decades, that it was hard to know when to insist, when to cajole him through necessary treatments, when to leave him to his own devices. He liked the serenity of his own company. He protested throughout that he was fine; he joked wryly about the asperities of his state. When I last saw him, he told me his only regret in life was that he had never travelled to Iceland, and he thought he could accept that minor deficit. His final words, ironically, were to insist that he was okay, and that we mustn't worry. I think by then he knew that it was over, his improbable longevity was drawing to an end; but the habit was so enduring, he couldn't abandon it.

When our parents die, when the loss falls hard and heavy upon us, we rebuke our former selves, but perhaps that isn't entirely fair. Often, after my father's death, I wished I could go back in time and tell my unwitting former self to stay with him, stay with him – he won't be here next week and you will miss him so profoundly, it will cause you physical pain. I had many decades to prepare for my father's death, and yet the completeness of the loss was shocking, all the same. Nothing prepares you for the blank finality of death. A new day dawns, and for a moment, as you emerge from sleep, you are confused, you think your father is still alive. Then, the brutal fact assails you, once again, and you feel as if you have been kicked in the guts. You are tormented by all the further questions you should have asked him – every day something occurs to you. And you are angry, really, about the immutable condition of mortality: that those we love must vanish in the end. Even our determined, kindly, much-loved and loving fathers.

When I think of my father now, I see him stooping in one doorway or another, a tall figure, six foot four, with thick curly hair that barely greyed. Driving great distances, quietly to dispense love, to me and my small children, his grandchildren, and then to vanish again. Onwards, for ever. Sometimes I think he is not dead at all, he's on one of his journeys, one more journey, of all the thousands of miles he covered. So you vacillate, between hope, and sorrow, and rough-hewn acceptance. My father died peacefully, and that is a consolation.

He once told me, after I had rather over-enthusiastically sent him a paperback version of my first book, when he had already loyally read and praised the hardback version, that he wanted me to dedicate the book again, and once more again, for luck. He was right, of course – we should dedicate our small enterprises, always, to our unique, irreplaceable fathers. Adapting the old poets, among them Catullus – *atque in perpetuum* . . . *ave atque vale.* So once again – with all my love, dear Father, and for ever – hail and farewell . . .

**Joanna Kavenna is the author of several
works of fiction and non-fiction.**

FOOTBALL HAS CAUSED MORE ARGUMENTS IN THE STEWART HOUSEHOLD THAN HITLER EVER COULD

Rob Stewart by Rod Stewart

During the war years, my dad was too old to serve so he was in the ARP, the Air Raid Precautions enforcers. I remember when I got older him telling me stories about going into children's hospitals that had been bombed. He had to go over to Highgate Wood and light huge fires with the ARP so that the Germans would think, Ooh, we've got a house here, let's bomb over there . . . It was dangerous work. In later years that's where I used to play football, which is a strange thought.

I was a bit of a mistake. As my brother tends to say, a very expensive mistake. My dad had come home one night and gone down the air-raid shelter . . . the Anderson Shelter, and, well . . .

Before I was born, my siblings – I've got two brothers and

two sisters – were asked to leave London and go and live in the country, like kids were at that age. All of them said, 'No, we want to stay with Mum and Dad.' We were in Highgate, so we didn't get bombed that much, but we still got bombed.

My dad was a hero to me because of his work ethic. He was a very proud Scotsman, too, although he only spent the first eighteen years of his life up in Scotland. He had to move down south to find work after a brief spell in the Merchant Navy.

I loved his football ethic, too. It was the same with me: football above everything. He broke his leg on Christmas Eve playing football and had to spend Christmas in hospital. My mum burnt his football boots! Football has caused more arguments in the Stewart household than Hitler ever could.

He gave me a lot of advice over the years that's stood me in good stead. When he was getting into his late eighties, he said, 'The one thing I didn't want to do was find myself pushing myself out of me chair.' He'd played football all of his life and his advice to me was 'Always keep your leg strong.' And I do. When the muscle that keeps the two parts of the knee apart goes, you've got bone on bone smacking together and that's when it hurts. But if you keep your leg strong, it keeps everything pulled apart and tight. It's a great bit of advice. Of course, he also gave me the proverbial 'Keep it in your trousers!' line.

He didn't say much. He wasn't a man of many words, but he was extremely loving. He was a good dad. I loved him.

Rod Stewart is a singer and songwriter who has recorded hits across five decades.

I CAUGHT A GLIMPSE OF DAD, GREY-FACED, TEETH GRITTED

Tam Doyle by Tom Doyle

In 2013 I wrote a book – about Paul McCartney in the seventies – and I dedicated it to my dad: 'To Thomas Corrigan Doyle, for fixing the plug onto that first record player and setting me on my way.' He was quietly chuffed, I reckon, and I didn't have to explain it to him. He knew exactly what I meant.

It was 1971, I was four and living with him and my mum and younger brother Brian in Ranelagh Road, Leytonstone. We'd moved there from Dundee – for what turned out to be only nine months, while my dad and his London mate Tony were running a nocturnal office-cleaning-cum-thieving business. Obviously the details are sketchy to me now, but my dad had somehow acquired a plug-less Dansette and for weeks I'd been entranced by it. Knowing this, Tony had given me a pile of singles he'd 'found in the bins' (God knows where they'd really come from). I was itching to play them. This urge peaked one day as Dad was trying to paper the hallway of our rented flat. 'So there's me,' he would say, when telling the story in later years, 'up and down this fucking ladder and you bugging me to get this record player going.'

Finally, he gave in, sorted the plug, and I was off, blasting out these magical 45s – the Beatles, Free, 'Twenty-Four Hours from Tulsa'. While I was spinning some great rattling single that I was later to discover was ska, there was a knock on our front door. 'Two lassies standing there,' Dad would remember. 'And they say, "Is there a Jamaican party going on?" I swung the door right open and showed them you sitting with that record player and said, "Yeah, sure, there it is."'

He was – pretty much – always tolerant and encouraging when it came to my obsession with music. Being honest, I think it baffled him a bit, but he went with it. Sometimes, even as a tiny kid, I must have seemed a bit of a stranger to him: me dreamy-headed, him more hard-boiled. We shared a name (I'm the fourth Thomas Doyle in our family), but we were completely different on many levels and on others very much the same.

He'd had a rough upbringing at the hands of a harsh mother. Her first husband, my dad's father, had died during the Second World War and her second had drunk heavily, probably to blot out her witchy tantrums. Growing up, my dad was clearly a smart lad, but his future was already mapped out for him: he was going to work in their grocery shop. There had been glimmers of something more romantic – the maternal side of the family were circus and carnival people and he'd tell me about learning how to perform somersaults off the back of a horse as a kid. But this tantalising possible future as a travelling acrobat was quickly snuffed by reality and the pursuit of cash.

Looking back, the hard physical violence he suffered at the

hands of his mother left him seeking some kind of approval from her, which he never got and which manifested itself in a lifelong drive to make money and prove his worth. Throughout his childhood he saw precious little maternal affection or support. He used to talk about the Catholic family of boys who lived next door and how, if he'd got into a fight with one of them, he'd come crying to his mum and she'd snap at him and tell him to get back out there and 'batter him'. If he did, he'd then have to fight the elder brother and then the brother above that, until he'd been truly battered himself. As me and my own brother grew up, often fighting wildly with each other, he sometimes treated us in that same tough, physical way. A thump on the ear, a smack on the back of the head.

At the same time, he was hilarious. You only have to look at pictures of us from the seventies to see what a loose, funny operation our family was. For a time, after he quit the grocery game, he worked as a bus conductor and would gently take the piss out of the old grannies, telling them he was a bit deaf and getting them to shout into his 'hearing aid' (a fag packet in his top pocket connected to a bit of string stuck in his ear). Most of the memories of my childhood are of laughing my arse off at his stories.

Dundee in the seventies was a hellishly tough place, though. In 1976, Dad bought a chip shop on a council estate, next door to a pub. Come chucking-out time on a Friday or Saturday night, the pissed locals would pile in and numerous fights would erupt. 'It was like the fucking Wild West,' he'd remember. I was normally home tucked up in bed when all of this was going on, but one night, for whatever reason, I was still there, probably eating my body weight in chips. Some drunk refused to pay for his pie supper and threw it at my dad's head. I was in the back shop and my mum tried to pull me away as my dad launched himself at this guy. I caught a glimpse of Dad, grey-faced, teeth gritted, whacking this drunk on the head with a heavy Indian club. The bloke kept hitting the wall and coming back at him. 'It took me three smacks with this club to get the fucker to go down,' he'd say. 'Then I realised he was bouncing off the Formica wall.'

The guy moaned to his mates that my dad had assaulted him. 'Nah,' they said, 'Tam wouldn't do that. He's a good lad.'

He was, but at the same time you wouldn't mess with him. In later years, he'd lament the fact that he was 'a bit hard with you and Brian'. But it was true. On two occasions, once with me, once with my brother, we'd run into the back shop moaning that we'd come off worst in a fight. My old man would pull out his air pistol and say, 'Go on then, get him with this.' I clearly remember pointing the pistol at a kid who was maybe a hundred yards away, thinking, I'd better hit him or my dad'll be pissed off with me. (I did shoot the kid, eventually, in the leg, and my proud father denied all knowledge of any air pistol when the guy's freaked-out parents came in to challenge him over it.) Only now, looking back, do I realise how utterly mental this all was.

Being a chip-shop owner hardwired my dad into the network of Italians living in Dundee and he really felt he was one of them – learning the language, being 'adopted' by an elderly couple called Teresa and Luigi, who basically became his surrogate parents, driving us 1,200 miles from Scotland to Lago Maggiore for a holiday in 1979. There he completely fell in love with Italy: the food, the culture, the music.

Then, in August 1982, my mum died in horrible circumstances. Dad was forty-one, I was fifteen, my brother twelve. We suffered something close to a collective nervous breakdown and, from here on in, became equals. Three lads sharing a flat on the ninth floor of a tower block. On Friday nights, it was my job to do the washing, in a clattering old twin-tub, and I used to ease some of the pain of this chore by sneaking out on the landing stairs to smoke a joint. One night Dad asked me where I'd been and I told him. 'Get yer dope oot then,' he said, and we got stoned together. That night he suffered from comedy short-term-memory lapses – three times he got up to put away the twin-tub that he'd already packed away – and we would both double up laughing about it for years.

Soon after this, he got together with his second wife, Heather. They made for a much better team than he and my mum ever were and I ended up with two stepbrothers, Jimmy and John. At the time Dad was working as a shop-to-shop salesman for a bakery and on Saturdays I was his 'van laddie', involving many light-fingered escapades, which ensured that I was very well paid for a sixteen-year-old. By then I was playing in four or five bands, buying drum kits and beatboxes and synths from the proceeds of our nefarious activities. He'd act as what he called my 'unpaid roadie', driving me to rehearsal rooms and gigs.

Down the years he always supported me, but worried about me, and often, I think, wondered what I was doing, in his words, 'fucking around' with music and then music journalism, when I started working for a magazine aged seventeen. In 1988, I basically ran away to work in London and, being different and the same (and prone to locking horns), I think the 470 miles between us preserved our relationship.

In the nineties, when the bakery firm he worked for started to go under, he hit a major depression. On my visits back home, I became his vodka-assisted therapist, drinking and talking with him into the early hours. In time, he got back on his feet, and he and Heather bought the bakery's failing flagship shop for a song and turned it around, before – and he *loved* this – eventually selling it back to the original owners at an enormous profit.

In our long and winding drunken discussions, as he hit his sixties he'd marvel at the strangeness of the modern world. Once, when he first had cable TV installed, he gave me a demonstration of how it worked, showing off his new toy, flicking up to the 'naughty channels' as my toes curled. He stopped at a gay pay-per-view channel. While no homophobe, it boggled his mind. 'See, there you go, Tommy. For a fiver I can watch some guy getting it up the chuff.' He laughed, taking a long dramatic lug on his fag. 'Now, when I was young, homosexuality was illegal.' He paused and I waited for the inevitable punchline. 'And you could smoke anywhere you wanted.'

He dearly loved his cigs and, even when he developed angina, refused to stop smoking. (I once bemoaned this fact to – of all of people – Spike Milligan during an interview and he said my dad was a 'weak prick'. Childhood *Goons* fan that Dad was, I decided not tell him.) I'd sometimes have a go at him about his unrelenting thirty-to-forty-a-day habit and he'd take a cool, defiant puff and say, 'Well . . . you've got to die of something.'

Last November I was in Dundee – dropping my bag off at his place, with an hour to spare between working appointments – when he pulled me into the kitchen. 'Look, I'm no' trying to worry you, but I've got a pain,' he said, gesturing to the left side of his chest. I told him it was probably just his angina, since he always refused to use his 'puffer'. Two months later, he was diagnosed with lung cancer.

A pretty much unrepentant smoker to the last, he took it on the chin. Even at the hospital consultations, his humour remained bulletproof. 'How are you feeling, Mr Doyle?' asked one doctor.

'Well,' Dad deadpanned, 'I seem to get dizzy any time I open my wallet.'

Later, when he was admitted to hospital for a course of radiotherapy, we got dirty looks for laughing on the cancer ward.

Over the winter I moved back to Scotland for nearly three months, and together the whole family nursed him. He died at home, two months after his seventy-third birthday, on Valentine's Day 2014, as we held a surreal, hysterical (in both senses), sickening and heartbreaking 'party' around him that was like a particularly warped Mike Leigh play. His funeral, a week later, was filled with tasteless jokes and soul-stirring operatic arias. We've still to decide what to do with his ashes. 'Put me in an egg timer,' he'd joked darkly. 'Keep me working.'

But I don't want to dwell on the bad stuff. I want to remember Dad sitting at his coffee table with his smokes and his 'voddy for the body', counting out his money from the shop, separating the notes into piles with such fetishistic care that a girl at the bank once asked him if he ironed them. Or standing with his elbow on the mantelpiece, slowly telling some outrageous story. Or arguing with me, his 'bleeding-heart liberal son', about some finer political point that he would always defeat me on.

I want to remember him as the tolerant, fascinated soul that he really was beneath all that working-class bravado and Scottish tough-man exterior. At heart, he was a sentimentalist. When I was four he took me to see Disney's *Pinocchio* at the cinema. Years later, he told me that every time he heard 'When You Wish Upon a Star', he tried hard not to blub. Guess what? Me too.

Once, we were looking through all of the old family pictures and his eyes started filling up. 'It just makes you think,' he said, 'this was your life.' Time and time again, he'd say to me and my brother, 'When I kick the bucket, they won't put a statue of me up in the city square. You guys are my statue.' That may be true. But, as much as I was laughing and crying as I wrote it, this story exists as a statue of some kind.

Tom Doyle lives in north London and has been writing about music and other stuff for thirty years.

HE BLACKENS PAGES EVERY SINGLE DAY OF HIS LIFE

Leonard Cohen by Adam Cohen

I've had a very normal relationship with my father, with the exception that he's terribly well known and, so it is said, one of the most important writers in his domain.

Like all sons, I have found the relationship has added layers to itself over time. There's only one layer of the relationship that I didn't have and that's the rebellion layer. I was either too unaware that I should've been experiencing it or he was simply spared it. These days, I find my relationship with him is just looking in a mirror and consulting with him. Hearing the timbre of his voice in my own. Body posture, mannerisms, ethics, morals, linguistics. All the deep imprintings that are there from either socio-genetics or, if you were to be cruel, you could say it was parroting. Whatever the reason, I throw my arms around the lifestyle I was given.

My father made a remarkable effort – and one that I am much more impressed with now as a family man myself – to remain in his children's lives despite a less-than-perfect split-up with my mother. I always saw him. He was always around. He always made gigantic efforts. There was even a time when he wasn't allowed on the property and to circumnavigate that he bought a trailer and put it at the T of where the dirt road of our house connected to the municipal road in the south of France. And we'd walk up the dirt road. A lot was imparted by that. From Los Angeles to the south of France was no small journey. We spent all our holidays with him. Every winter we would go to Montréal and every summer we'd go to Greece.

There was always laughter. Despite his notoriety for, I quote, 'having a voice like the bottom of an ashtray', for being 'the prince of darkness', for being famed for his lugubriousness, he is one of the most quick-witted of men, and he's generous with his humour. The guy is hilarious. I've gone into the family business and we get a tremendous amount of laughter out of that. Also, talking about life and women and the journey we're all on, that brings me so much joy. Hanging out with him is the best, whether it's over a tuna sandwich or on the front stoop of his house. He doesn't like to move much, having been a touring man his whole life. He does love being sedentary.

I've learnt a lot from him on that stoop. The main inspiration that his life provides is a dedication to his craft. He has an old-world view of it. It's not the prevalent notion that exists in new generations of instantaneous success. His whole life has been a demonstration in the opposite. I remember something he told me when I was sixteen and starting to take songwriting seriously. He said there's a moment when you're blocked on a song, or on any work, and it's only when you're about to quit having put much, much more time than you planned into it that the work begins. That's when you've crossed the threshold of being on the right track. But the nature of my dialogue with him is nearly always instruction. From the manner in which we should greet someone about whom we have reservations, to gender relationships, to the proper dosage of mustard and mayonnaise. We talk about women all the time, too, and, if I may, out of privacy, I'll keep that princely wisdom to myself. It is a long-running and possibly incomplete transmission.

We visited him often when he lived in a Zen Buddhist monastery in the nineties. He would periodically come down off the mountain. Whatever residue there was from his studies was always apparent to us. Like a halo. Like a film of something we knew was other-worldly. A calmness, a peace, a clarity. All of which he's tried to impart to us, not always with great success.

I love seeing him at work. I'm still tingling with pride that this man's return to the stage was so triumphant, so reverberant, so ministerial, so sermon-like, so moving. All you have to do is consult a review in any of the papers in any of the countries where he performed. He was referred to as the Sistine Chapel of live music. I mean . . . That seems like hyperbole or inflated praise, but I was moved to tears by the beauty of this man standing on the heap of his work and offering it with such generosity, such precision, such mastery. The Greeks came up with nostalgia, and it's two words: *nostos*, which is memory, and *algos*, which is pain. That's beautiful. And I experience a premature nostalgia whenever I think about my dad.

We've never really fallen out. We've had a series of minor misunderstandings that were corrected and actually served to provide better understanding in the long run. When you have someone in your family who is in such demand and whom you derive a sense of identity from because of the nature of your own relationship, then you can start to become covetous of the amount of time spent with the person. There are times when, no question, I wish we'd gotten to spend more time together.

But the time we have spent together is so valuable. I've been to so many great parties and events with him. I remember he was doing a big show in Paris and Sarkozy and Carla Bruni were backstage afterwards. He said to me, 'Anything that anybody says to me, I want you to answer on my behalf. I want the President of France to know that I've brought up fully Francophone children.' It was a badge of pride for him.

Now I have my own son and while it's difficult to say for sure if a seven-year-old resembles his grandfather, certainly a love of languages is there. Judaism, too. Not that it plays a huge role in our life, but just last Friday we were having one of our regular family meals at a Greek restaurant to light the seven candles as a family. To see my son reading Hebrew and being the chairman of prayers at the table . . . I didn't do that and I know that was something my father regretted. For my son to rectify that and to witness the pride it provides for my father is beautiful.

You want to know some secrets about Leonard Cohen? Here's the dirt. He loves George Jones and Hank Williams. He travels with one small suitcase. Many of his impeccable suits are actually threadbare. He's only about five foot eight despite that giant baritone. He awakens at four in the morning and blackens pages every single day of his life. He cuts his own hair. He will find a patch of sun anywhere and sit in it, like a big cat, following that sliver of sun wherever it goes. Although he no longer smokes, there's nothing he'd rather do. He makes the best tuna salad I've ever had – he seems to have a knack for that. He loves making food for people, in fact. He spends a lot of time in the kitchen. Leonard Cohen's probably the best-known short-order chef in the world.

**Adam Cohen is a singer and songwriter.
He lives in Los Angeles.**

I DISCOVERED DAD'S 'SECRET' HAD SHAPED HIS CHARACTER

Charlie Catchpole by Charlie Catchpole

My lovely gentle dad never once raised his hand to me. Come to think of it, he hardly ever raised his voice. I can recall only one occasion when I saw him really, really angry. I was about eight and Dad had taken the family to look over the house that was to become my childhood home, on a smart little estate of newly built 'desirable dwellings' just outside King's Lynn in Norfolk. Dad was so proud. It was the first house he'd ever bought and seen rise from its foundations. Until then, we'd lived in a succession of shabby rented houses and flats wherever his job in the lower reaches of the civil service took him.

Now he'd been promoted to manage the local office of what was then the National Assistance Board – later the DHSS. He was in his early forties, he had a decent salary and he wanted to put down roots. (Why this was so important to him, I didn't discover till some years later.) Anyway, when he opened the front door of the half-completed building, he was astonished to discover a man and a woman sitting on the stairs drinking tea from a Thermos flask. The man jumped to his feet and hastily explained they were passing by, it had started to rain, so they decided to take shelter. 'Not in my house you don't!' shouted Dad.

Even now, some sixty years later, I can vividly see him snatching the stranger's flask from his hands and hurling it down on to the scruffy beige raincoat on which the couple had parked their considerable backsides. Hot tea was sprayed everywhere. The strangers legged it, sharpish. Dad slammed the door shut behind them, shouting rude words I'd never heard him utter before.

My sister and I gawped at each other in amazement. This wasn't like Dad at all.

He was fit and sporty then – as a schoolboy he'd been an accomplished boxer and he still played cricket and football. But physical, even verbal, violence simply wasn't his way. Dad served in the army in the hell-hole that was Burma during the Second World War – he was a sergeant in the Intelligence Corps – and I imagined he must have seen some terrible things. But he never once talked about his wartime experiences. The only oblique reference he ever made was when I discovered a fearsome-looking jack-knife among the spanners and screwdrivers in his toolbox in the garage.

'That was for cutting Japs' ears off,' he said matter-of-factly. I assumed he was joking, but I couldn't be sure. With Dad, you never knew.

When we were older, my sister – who was always the more perceptive of the two of us – said she felt he was repressed and this was a source of constant frustration to Mum. He came from a generation that didn't believe in 'letting it all hang out'. Dad was the very personification of the stiff-upper-lip

Englishman. I never saw him shed a tear over anything and I honestly cannot remember him ever hugging me or telling me he loved me. That sort of thing just wasn't in his make-up. Not that I was particularly bothered. I knew he must love me. Dad wasn't cold or stand-offish at all. He was a kind and generous man. But he kept himself to himself.

Mum, on the other hand, was a fiercely spirited woman with a short fuse and a filthy temper. She regularly whacked me – no complaints, I always deserved it – and more than once I remember her sending me to bed early and issuing that classic warning: 'Just wait till your father gets home!

It was the emptiest of threats.

Dad might come up and have a little chat about my misbehaviour, but I knew I had nothing to fear. His placid, plodding nature must have driven Mum mad. I often heard them arguing downstairs – or, rather, I heard her yelling at him. Once, terrifyingly, came the sound of the front door slamming late at night. She'd walked out, in a rage. Many years later, Mum told me she'd become so angry over some long-forgotten trifling matter that she'd thrown a book at him. It caught him above the eye and drew blood. Dad never mentioned it.

Many years later, I discovered Dad's 'secret', which I realised had shaped his character. He was illegitimate. In those days – he was born in 1911 – to his 'respectable' lower-middle-class family, this was a source of great shame. My dad's mother, I eventually learned from Mum, was 'in service' at some grand mansion in the Norfolk countryside.

As a teenager she'd got pregnant, and her lover – I fancifully imagined it was the master of the house – had eloped with her to London, where Dad was born in the Whitechapel Hospital. The man promptly did a runner. All Dad knew was that his name was Wilson and he was subsequently believed to have died in the First World War. Dad was taken back to

Norfolk and raised by his grandmother and a couple of aunts.

His childhood was not a particularly happy one, but neither was it especially unhappy. However, placed in the care of older women, he missed out on all those precious father-and-son moments, like fishing expeditions and going to football matches. Instead, he threw himself into his studies and earned a place at a well-regarded grammar school in Norwich.

Money was tight in Dad's adoptive all-female 'family', and I've long thought it was this spartan upbringing that informed his socialist beliefs. He always voted Labour, and Harold Wilson – Labour's first prime minister since the year dot – was his hero. Not surprisingly, Dad was vehemently opposed to public schools, which he saw as bastions of privilege. But his views were tested to the limit when I somehow passed my eleven-plus with distinction and was offered a scholarship as a boarder at a minor public school in Suffolk. There was no argument now. Dad was adamant: if I wanted to go, I should go.

Bastion of privilege or not, the school offered a better all-round education than I could expect at the distinctly average local grammar. Dave Larter, an England fast bowler of the day, had been a pupil there. Dad was quite impressed by that. And I really did want to go, so I went. In a heartbeat, my dad had sacrificed his long-held political principles for my sake.

That's how much he loved me.

Charlie Catchpole is a Fleet Street journalist and columnist on the *Sunday People*.

IT IS GOOD TO DANCE, IN VERY SHORT SHORTS, IN THE SUMMERTIME

Barry Wood by Anna Wood

Some things I've learned from my dad.

Read books. Surround yourself with books. Life will be better, you will be better, everything will be better. Words are yours.

It is good to dance, in very short shorts, in the summertime, along the beach at Sutton-on-Sea, singing 'Blame It on the Boogie'.

It is good to dance, in the kitchen, to 'Crocodile Rock'. (It may never be as good again as when I was very little and standing on my dad's feet, holding his hands, while we danced in the kitchen to 'Crocodile Rock'.)

Sit at the kitchen table doing the crossword with a loved one, or read out clues while the loved one makes tea. You can do this a few times a week, for years, for decades, and it will always be a good idea.

Loyalty is a good idea. But don't put up with wankers. Laugh at them gently, fondly, and then walk away.

The main thing about living in a detached house is you can play your music louder.

Read poetry, listen to it, memorise it. Poetry pursues the human like the smitten moon above the weeping, laughing earth. I spit the pips, and feel the drunkenness of things being various. See into the life of things. 'Moon!' you cry suddenly. 'Moon! Moon!'

Whisky is good. Scotch, usually, with a splash of cold water. It is best late at night (or early in the morning) with friends and conversation.

And cheese, and crusty bread.

Good shoes. Cool shoes.

And jazz. Maybe even opera, one day.

You're all right.

Other people are interesting.

Kindness is strength.

Have a good cry if you need one. And a hug.

Anna Wood writes short stories.

HE DEALS EXCLUSIVELY IN PERCENTAGES

John Deevoy by Adrian Deevoy

My father is not a great man. He has never, to my knowledge, liberated hollow-cheeked, khaki-shorted men from Japanese death camps or flown in a fighter jet or anything other than a comfy Airbus. He's not had a sniff of the Nobel Peace Prize and hasn't ever made a speech, other than the one he gave me about poofs who wear patchouli.

But my dad is a great bloke. He's funny, profound and charismatic, and pathologically unable to take life seriously. Like a rogue Terry Wogan, he enjoys the craic and everyone loves him for it. He's got friends in high places and plenty more downstairs by the pool tables.

Reared in rural Ireland, conveniently close to Portlaoise prison, the third youngest of, I think, seventy-one siblings, he sometimes rode to school on a donkey and didn't see a black man until he was fourteen. The Afro'd stranger trundled through the village on a bicycle and all the local children

153

followed him, 'like he was an African Pied Piper . . . on a bike'.

Dad was educated by Christian Brothers who, while doing God's work, regularly beat their pupils unconscious. If that doesn't prepare you for life's sadists, rapists and sickos, nothing will.

He put the experience to good use and worked in a massive mental hospital for half his adult life.

At a time when psychiatric illness was frowned upon, even feared, Dad didn't discriminate, knowing full well that he 'probably wasn't the full shilling either'. He got on famously with the patients, some of them murderers and worse.

One man had invented his own language and often admitted himself to the local maternity wing in the belief that he was about to give birth to the son of God. A bearded character named Joe told me he was controlled by the radio waves emitted by Jimi Hendrix's guitar and Tony Blackburn's Sunday lunchtime show. Another woman, Vivienne, frequently set herself on fire and had flecks of fabric scorched into her skin. They all became family friends.

So, I grew up surrounded by the mentally disturbed and went on to work in the music business – I swear I'll write a book about it one day.

It would be a safe bet to say my dad enjoys gambling. In fact, he deals exclusively in percentages. Everything from the Ryder Cup to a comment about your haircut is a calculation. He once kept a record of his bets over a ten-year period, big wins, bad losses, and came out around thirty pounds down. No wonder my mum couldn't stand it any more. I spent the tail end of my teenage years refereeing my parents' imminent divorce.

It had always been a mismatch. Mum with her head in a book by R. D. Laing, Dad with his in a barmaid's blouse. That they stayed together for twenty years was a minor miracle.

They'd met at the Hammersmith Palais de Danse. Mum could never quite remember what she saw in him but it certainly wasn't his dansing. When they married in Shepherd's Bush in the early sixties, Dad was younger than Sid Vicious ever got to be. Like Sid, he fought Teddy Boys in Ladbroke Grove and befriended disenfranchised Jamaicans, albeit back in the days when the notorious 'No Blacks, No Irish, No Dogs' sign would hang on boarding-house doors. He drank in pubs, some of which still stand today, the last bastions of non-gastrification: the Crown and Sceptre, the Coningham, the White Horse. Boozers I have known since I could barely see over a bag of crisps.

As a child I believed that my father had been an Icelandic fisherman. He told terrifying tales of his time trawling the savage North Sea, where strong sailors, good men, died in cold so severe that he didn't notice losing three fingers from his left hand.

I stopped my sympathetic sobbing to ask how come he still had the discontinued digits. 'They grew back,' he bullshitted bullishly, then ploughed on with his heartbreaking story.

In terms of learning, my dad once spent a valuable afternoon patiently teaching me to spit properly. It has served me well and I can still hit a wad of gum into a urinal from twenty paces. He also told me that I am not a drop in the ocean but the whole of the ocean in one drop. That bogus piece of cod philosophy has seen me through a few grim times, I can tell you.

In 1974, he dabbled with disciplinarianism but would often be undermined by his own behaviour. I once brought a gaggle of stoned friends home only to find a trail of my father's clothes leading up the stairs to the master bedroom, where he was making uninhibited love to my mother. At least, I think it was my mother. One of my drug buddies, Excitable Stan, literally pissed himself laughing.

Years later, I was with a girlfriend in my own room engaged in a similar act of physical affection when I felt a sharp slap on my bare behind. 'Hurry up,' chirped my well-refreshed father. 'There's a queue of us waiting out here.'

He was and remains the kind of dangerous dad that your contemporaries adored. He'd often answer the door to them in his horrible underpants, if they were lucky, clutching a claw hammer and dribbling for dramatic effect.

He had a neat way with a self-deprecating Irish one-liner. His burgeoning beer gut was always 'relaxed muscle'. Less-than-pretty people had 'trodden on a few rakes'. He will routinely tell you that he doesn't drink any more 'but I don't drink any less'.

Dad met his second wife at her first husband's funeral with the immortal chat-up line 'Well, you're single now . . .' Cherie fell for him on the spot. 'Cheeky swine,' she swooned.

When she died young I thought he'd fall apart, but he pulled through, by delighting in the life they'd shared together. He'd lost his soul-mate, his lioness, but his rationale was that at least he had found her in the first place.

He has always rolled with the punches, fallen on his feet and relied on his dubious Irish charm. Even when some unenlightened soul daubed 'IRA Pigs' on our house, at the height of the Troubles, Dad – in an attempt to distance himself from terrorism – claimed not to be able even to spell IRA.

Did you ever have a dream that you couldn't explain? I once took Dad to see Dylan at Wembley Stadium. He headed straight for the free drinks and started skulling Guinness like a drought had been announced. Knowing what would happen, I left him to it and went to watch the altogether more predictable Jewish singer.

I returned after the encores to find Dad deep in conversation with the actor Dennis Waterman, offering sloshed advice on his faltering marriage with Rula Lenska. They split up shortly afterwards.

At another party in the mid-eighties, I introduced Dad to the flamboyant but troubled singer Adam Ant. By the time I'd got back from the bar, Adam was cheerily calling my dad 'Paddy Ant', as they animatedly discussed the combustible nature of lunatic asylums. They got on like a nuthouse on fire.

Dad recently had a double stroke: bleed at the front, big burst at the back. The hospital called to say he was unsteady on his feet and his speech was slurred. 'Nothing new there, then,' I quipped, then vomited with anxiety.

Upon reaching the Intensive Stroke Unit, I expected to see a haunted shadow of a man, but he was in reliably robust form, propped on his pillows, perusing the lunch menu, winding up a sweet old Gujarati gent in the opposite bed whom Dad had decided to call Gandhi.

The strokes had left Dad unable to remember the word for 'stroke'. He called them 'scones'.

'I was okay till I had those feckin' scones,' he'd say. It led to a pleasurable afternoon of bakery-based, rupture-related punning. But that's me and my dad – where the pun never sets. It can't be good for the old 'jam tart'.

A Nigerian nurse came around to take some blood for further tests.

'When do you think I should tell him about the Aids?' Dad asked innocently.

But the 'scones' were serious, so – as ever in times of emotional stress – we talked not of life's fragility or the final whisper being wrung from the yew, but about Queen's Park Rangers. It was good to hear Dad's familiar ''Arry's having a laugh' refrain again.

Having been born in Shepherd's Bush, I had little choice but to support QPR. Dad took me to Loftus Road when I was too impressionable to understand a world beyond Stan Bowles's insouciant sorcery and Dave Thomas's defiantly rolled-down socks.

I still call Dad before every home game, from outside the ground, just prior to kick-off and we have a comfort-moan about the Rs. He likes to hear the disgruntled hubbub in the background and reckons he can smell the onions from the hot-dog vans. Dad doesn't go any more: he knows Rangers are rubbish.

When he had his strokes, we joked about lumping on at the bookie's for a dead Dad/Rangers relegation double. A healthy dose of humour always helps, I find.

And as the clock on the wall laughs at us all, I can see QPR going down but, God willing, the world's greatest bloke will survive another season.

Adrian Deevoy has been writing about music since 1978. He lives in London and elsewhere.

'WHY ARE YOU LISTENING TO GREEN DAY? YOU WANNA BE LISTENING TO THE RAMONES'

Nick Welch by Florence Welch

My dad's incredibly emotional and sensitive. He's a very louche, swearing, fairy-like creature. I always felt like he was waiting for my sister and me to grow up so he could hang out with us. 'You're babies, you're babies, you're babies . . . Ah! You're teenagers! Excellent! Would you like a glass of wine?' He just wanted some accomplices he could trust.

A thin, elegant, smoking man: he was always very charming and my idol growing up. I've spent my whole life trying to impress him. After school musicals he'd shower me with faint praise. 'Wonderful, darling, not your best performance, but fantastic.' But then he became my biggest supporter and he even tour-managed us. He drove us around Europe in his camper-van when we supported MGMT. I think me becoming a performer was enjoyable for him because he's definitely a rock 'n' roll dad.

The scariest thing that happened was that he got hit on

his bike when I was in New York, on tour. He was drunk at the time. His bike was mangled, and when he woke up he couldn't remember what had happened. He got checked out by my stepdad, who is a doctor, and everyone thought he was fine. The next morning, however, he woke up and believed he was still married to my mother. They'd been divorced for about ten years. He had bleeding in his brain. That was terrifying. I'm so attached to him, I love my dad so much and the thought . . . But he's fine now. Part of that fear is to do with his physique, I think. He's almost bird-like, and that always made me and my sister feel unreasonably ravenous, as if he'd given birth to these enormous hungry cuckoos, constantly flapping about dramatically and demanding pizza.

I'm not alone in loving my dad this much. Everyone does. He's a legend. He's the manager of an organic campsite, which sounds modest, but he always makes me regretful of my own education. I remember a lot of my childhood would be me asking questions, and he could speak so eloquently on any subject, in fluent French if necessary. He introduced me to the Smiths and the Rolling Stones. The Velvet Underground. He'd come into my room and say, 'Why are you listening to Green Day? You wanna be listening to the Ramones.' He used to run squat parties where Joe Strummer's 101ers would play. All of that stuff.

He's sensitive and deliciously rude. He's still the most well-dressed man. The most fantastic cook as well. Fuck, my dad's great.

Florence Welch is the singer with Florence + the Machine.

HALF-TRUTHS, RUMOURS AND SECOND-HAND MEMORIES

Harry Doherty by Niall Doherty

The first time I ever saw my dad was when my mum laid down a copy of the *Derry Journal* in front of me. I was nine years old and sitting at the dinner table in our flat in Walthamstow. She opened up the paper and there he was, his words, his face, looking back at me. It was a special anniversary edition of the *Journal* and, as one of their ex-writers who'd gone on to Great Things, he'd written an article about his time there. I went into a sort of panicked shock. I read it five times in a row and then bawled my eyes out.

My dad had left when I was six months old. In my life, we've had two main phases of contact with each other. If I hold up all my fingers in front of me, that's about the amount of times I've met him, so you'll have to excuse this piece being mostly made up of half-truths, rumours and second-hand memories. There are some of my own recollections scattered here and there.

Harry Doherty was born in Derry in the 1950s. The son of a milkman, he was a teenager as Northern Ireland's civil-rights movement was kicking off. He and my mum were on the Bloody Sunday march; it's him at the front of the stock footage the BBC show every time they mention it – he'd gone to the front as he was covering it for the *Journal*. Later, he started writing about music and they moved to London. By the mid-seventies, he was one of the main writers at *Melody Maker*. He was one of the first people to write about Kate Bush and he wrote extensively on Thin Lizzy, although I think he balanced this out by also writing an awful lot about Jethro Tull. I write about music for a living too (you can have that one for free) and can only imagine the big-collared, flares-wearing fun of living the *Almost Famous* dream. It was an era that invented rock 'n' roll clichés, and he probably did most of them; he told me that he'd done heroin 'by accident', thinking it was coke. My cousin once let slip that my dad was sleeping with one of Abba and that was one of the reasons why they split. I have no idea if that's true, although I found it hard to join in the celebrations of his legendary swordsmanship.

When I was eleven, he got in touch for the first time. My mum took me to meet him at Earl's Court Tube and we went to a computer-games exhibition. He looked like me, except his hair was completely white and he was quite fat. He gave me a copy of U2's *Achtung Baby* and Pearl Jam's *Ten*. The next time we met, he took me to Southend-on-Sea. We had fish and chips and then we drove in his Mercedes Benz to a printing house so he could check up on how production was going on *Metal Hammer*, the newly launched hard-rock magazine he was the editor of. He gave me some more CDs: *Nevermind* by Nirvana, *Yerself Is Steam* by Mercury Rev and something by the Hothouse Flowers. He also gave me a copy of *Metal Hammer*, which came with a giant *Nevermind* poster that I stuck on my wall as soon as I got home. These are mostly the bands that shaped the music I listened to then and have ever since, apart from Hothouse Flowers. Another time, he took me to *Metal Hammer*'s offices. I was at an impressionable age, and with all the CDs lying around and posters on the wall, it's not hard to remember what made me excited about the idea of working at a music magazine.

My mum was pleased that I was happy about seeing him, but it was a short-lived phase of communication. I had his home phone number and one night I called to speak to him. A girl answered, then my dad spoke to me quickly and asked to be handed over to my mum. He bollocked her for letting me call the house. The girl who answered was my younger sister, who, like her younger brother, had no idea I existed. Things petered out after that. I remember my mum looking so sad one night when he didn't show for a school assembly I was singing at. I think she felt it was her fault for exposing me, which really wasn't fair on my lovely mum. There were a few exchanges by letter after that. In one, I told him he'd let me down. In the response, he opened with this: 'There are three sides to every story: his, hers and the truth.' It was a play on an album title, *III Sides to Every Story*. His way of explaining the situation to me was by citing the work of Boston funk-metal group Extreme.

Ten years later, I was just about to finish university in Leicester. I hadn't had any contact with him in a very long time. But I'd really started to feel a weight on my shoulders about it. I was worried that if something were to happen to him, I'd feel guilty for not getting in touch. I knew that was absurd but, like a lot of absurd thoughts, it just wouldn't shift. I googled him, found his email and wrote to him before rationale had a chance to stop me. We exchanged emails for a while, then met up in December 2002 and went for a pizza in Kensington. I was now old enough to drink my way through any awkwardness, and as I was working at a music magazine myself, he told me stories about how it used to be. We would do this maybe once or twice a year. It felt fine, adult even. I'd scratched my itch.

My mum died in 2007 after a decade-long battle with cancer. I was absolutely heartbroken. She was an amazingly cool and profoundly kind person. After that, I just lost interest in the whole Dad thing. I don't know if that was a reaction to the fact I couldn't see my mum any more, or if I'd realised I didn't need a dad. Maybe a bit of both. It seemed like the less interested I became in maintaining any sort of relationship with him, the harder he tried. He would email me asking for photos of his granddaughter, trying to arrange a meet-up, and probably banging his head against a brick wall due to the lack of replies.

In 2013, I wrote a piece about him for My Old Man, the blog that birthed this book. He saw it and emailed me about it. I focused on the obvious fact he'd been googling himself. We were on a plane together shortly after to go to Ireland for his mother, my grandmother's funeral and we talked about it. He told me he was angry when he'd first read it but a friend of his had said something along the lines of 'Isn't that what happened, though?' So he read it again, and recognised a past he'd never really faced up to. He'd gone through life not paying much attention to consequences but here were his actions laid bare on a blog he'd stumbled upon.

A few months later, I visited him in hospital as a long-standing stomach problem had got much worse. As soon as I saw him, I knew he wouldn't be leaving. He could hardly talk and I sat next to him for ten minutes or so, barely saying anything myself. As I left, I patted him gently on the shoulder and said something stupid like 'Be good.' There was nothing left to say, no bedside grieving, no emotional outpourings.

Everything I ever wanted to say was in the piece I'd written, in the piece he'd read, and we both knew it. He died a few days later. It was over, a father and son forever out of time. The moment had passed.

Niall Doherty is a music writer from London. He lives in Southend with his wife and two children.

I COULD SEE MY OWN FACE IN THE GLASS'S REFLECTION

Howard Ross by Adam Ross

It happened that my father and I ended up in Los Angeles together.

This was in 2002, and I was there to interview Reese Witherspoon. Back then, I was writing for the *Nashville Scene*, my adopted city's alternative weekly. Witherspoon, a Nashville native, had, out of respect for a local writer, bequeathed me a whole half-hour of her press junket – making me feel both small-time and small-town. This was exacerbated by the fact that I was on a shoestring budget. Along with the cheap hotel, my editor had allowed me to rent a car, but only on the condition that I go economy, in size as well as price, and driving around Los Angeles in a Dodge Neon had dimmed the event's glamour. I was excited, don't get me wrong, but I also felt like an impostor, like I didn't belong with the *Vanity Fair* and *New York Times* reporters, and never would. The novel and short-story collection I'd been working on for a decade, the books that I'd promised my wife and sworn to myself would catapult me out of anonymity, not to mention earn me work in national publications, remained unfinished. My marriage was suffering from this and my meagre prospects. I was living with the constant possibility that I'd ruined my life.

Meanwhile, Dad had flown in from New York to move his ninety-one-year-old mother into a nursing home. She'd been a widow for nearly a quarter of a century and had, until recently, remained doggedly independent. Part of this was a result of her being social: she made a daily four-bus commute to meet friends for a muffin and coffee. But a year ago she'd been hit by a car when she was crossing the street, and the accident, which had broken her legs and hip, had left her physically incapable of living alone. There were also small but telling signs that her mind was starting to fail: her attention faded out, like a weak radio signal; she occasionally forgot her grandchildren's names; she regularly neglected to eat and, sometimes, bathe. 'I spoke to your grandmother the other day,' my father might mention when he called me. 'I think she's getting near the end.' He made this grim prediction with a tone that was close to hope. She was burning through her humble savings. MediCal and Social Security would cover only so much of her assisted-living expenses, the difference my father feared he'd soon have to cover at a time when he was financially vulnerable. Plus his feelings toward her remained ambivalent at best.

My father's extended family resided in Los Angeles: his mother's sister, her husband, and Uncle Ted, and various now grown-up children. And, of course, there was his mother, Miriam. She and her husband, Morris, had moved from Middle Village, Queens, in 1954 to start a fur-coat business, this on the same day my father returned from his tour in the navy. According to my father, his parents had met him in their car on 34th Street, in front of Macy's, to say goodbye before making the drive across the country. They gave him two hundred dollars – the only money they ever would – then left him to start their lives anew. My grandfather's business was a success but cut short because of his precipitously declining health and eventual death, in 1975, of a brain tumour. I had no memory of my grandfather, and could count the number of times my grandmother had visited with us, or we with her, on one hand. So far as my father was concerned, the whole California clan had abandoned him. He never said this directly, although he spoke of Los Angeles with spite. 'I hate it there,' he'd declare, and then add, with a New Yorker's condescension, 'Everyone lives in their car.'

My father was an actor. Up until the early eighties he'd performed in Broadway musicals – he was a gifted vocalist – but made the lion's share of his money doing commercial voiceovers, a lucrative gig if you can break into the cabal of actors who can engagingly deliver tag-lines and brought-to-you-bys in twenty-eight-to-sixty-second spots. At his apogee, his voice was ubiquitous, especially in the nineties, when MTV was in full effect and cable was proliferating.

But commercial actors are the economy's canaries in the coal mine, and whenever a recession hits, advertising budgets are the first to be cut. The past year had been terrible and no end was in sight.

I make it sound as if my father were a failure, when in fact nothing could be further from the truth. On Broadway, he had worked with some of the biggest names in the business – with Alan Jay Lerner, Leonard Bernstein and Joshua Logan. He'd voice-coached actors such as Lauren Bacall, Anthony Quinn and Barbara Harris. In what remains to me an act of pure nerve, he'd supported a family in New York City as a freelancer, never knowing on Monday where he'd get paid by Friday, putting my brother and me through private school and college,

173

building a house in the Hamptons, buying an apartment on the Upper West Side. But there were times such as these when his entire livelihood seemed in jeopardy, when the fact, as he had observed, that there was 'no graduation system in this business' seemed inescapably true.

The day before my Witherspoon interview, my father and I met Uncle Ted and my grandmother to take her to lunch. She wasn't in a good way, physically or emotionally. She was weepy and felt like she was now a burden to her family. She cried over her eggs and toast, which she barely touched. 'I'm ready for this all to be over,' she said. 'I'm ready to die.' She'd shrunk below five feet. She was incapable of making eye contact. It was early September and she wore a heavy sweater: she couldn't stay warm. Uncle Ted grew exasperated with her but my father seemed especially harsh. 'It's *not* over,' my father said. 'You're going to be well taken care of!' Afterward, he and I drove her home.

My grandmother's apartment was drab, a small place in West Hollywood whose furnishings looked like a set from the fifties. The television was one of those bureau-sized black-and-white models with a separate UHF knob and a domed screen that looked as thick as a hockey rink's Plexiglas. Her radio was also enormous, as big as a toaster, with yellow fabric covering its speaker. Her refrigerator, which had one of those latch-pull handles, was practically empty. There wasn't a book in the house – my grandmother, who had fled the pogroms of Russia and Poland, had had only an elementary-school education.

There was, however, a wall full of framed photographs in her living room and one in particular caught my eye. It was of my father in his early twenties, a professional headshot, taken in a studio. He was wearing a turtleneck and holding a pipe – an absurd prop because he had never smoked in his life; he looked like a Jew trying to dress as a WASP. I should mention that my father and I are nearly identical in appearance, and as I gazed on his image I could see my own face in the glass's reflection and suffered, in turn, my oldest fear, grounded in that very concrete conclusion that comes from resembling a parent: that I, too, would suffer my father's fate, be doomed to repeat his life somehow. He had signed it, 'To my mother: May all your silver screen dreams for me come true!' They had not. He'd never been in a single movie. As for my own artistic aspirations, these, too, seemed as misguided as my father's costume. I had one of the most powerful epiphanies I'd ever experienced: You can mistake passion for talent, hope for ability, then spend your entire life chasing a goal you were never equipped to achieve in the first place.

I left to go and prepare for my interview but my father remained behind. To save money, he was spending the night on his mother's couch.

I showed up to the junket early, with over two hours' worth of questions, which I'd run by our paper's film critic *ad nauseam*. I'd seen all of Witherspoon's movies and had taken extensive notes on each. I checked and triple-checked my laptop's power supply, my Dictaphone's readiness. 'Testing,' I said into its mike, this just like my father before he recorded a spot. 'Testing one, two, three.'

In person, Witherspoon was lovely and unselfconscious. The half-hour flew by but I came away from it relieved. I'd gotten the material I felt like I needed.

That night, I took my dad to see the press screening.

He was as relieved as I to be sitting in a movie theatre, but for very different reasons. He had spent the day looking at assisted-living facilities, confronting all of their attendant spectres of mortality as well as his own financial anxieties and now, more than anything, what he wanted to do was lose himself in a film. Since he was a boy movies had been a great relief to him, and tonight was no exception.

Afterwards, we went to the Palm. I offered to pay, and my father accepted, with the agreement that we'd each order an appetiser, then split a steak. It was a meal I couldn't really afford at the time, but it was my pleasure. Sometimes you need to spend money you don't have. It's an act of rebellion against circumstance, a fuck-you to Fate.

I have a very clear memory of the steak, which was a New York strip. The waiter sliced it for us before serving, then set it between our plates. It was cooked perfectly: pink straight through, the meat almost silky in appearance and laid out like fallen dominoes in its own juices. The restaurant was jammed and, to all concerned, my father and I looked like we belonged, and for a while we forgot that we didn't, and although this was enormously cheering, even more so was the recognition that neither of us was alone on our respective paths. We were men who had chosen difficult careers. I'd go back to Nashville and struggle to launch mine while he'd return to New York and fight to keep his. We didn't know what the future would bring (my grandmother, it's worth noting, would live for another decade) but right here, right now, we were keeping each other company, replenishing ourselves, gathering up strength for the next push. We left the restaurant feeling full.

Adam Ross is a novelist. He lives in Nashville.

HE BUST MY NOSE ON STAGE AT WEMBLEY

Derek Ryder by Shaun Ryder

My old bloke didn't stop competing with me until I was forty. But now he's seventy-three he's calming down. He doesn't move out of the house any more. He just sits watching movies, smoking weed.

He started off as a postman and he did that job so that he could finish at eleven o'clock in the morning, then go out and either be a stand-up comedian or play in the Irish clubs with his accordion and banjo, or go over to the country-and-western clubs, just to earn a tenner. He was pretty funny and he's one of those people who could turn his hand to anything. I can't really play instruments. Our Paul was the instrument player. I can work something out so I can get a tune in my head, but my dad could pick up any instrument and be playing it in five minutes.

When Happy Mondays took off he started working with us. First of all he was managing us and then, when it got to the stage where it was beyond him, he became the sound man, the tech, the roadie, all mixed in one. He worked with me like that for twenty-odd years, but it totally ruined my relationship with him for a long time afterwards. It came to a head when I played Wembley one time. I was shouting at him to sort out the monitors and in front of ten thousand people he walks in front of me and smacks me. He bust my nose! Our manager had to sack him. I was mortified.

We didn't speak for years. By the time we'd spent twenty years together on the road we couldn't talk for a long time, but now we can. In the last five years we've started being pals again. Time heals. He's a great old geezer.

Shaun Ryder is a singer from Manchester whose groups have included Happy Mondays and Black Grape.

HIS LIFE WAS BUILT AROUND PEOPLE NOT COMING BACK

Alfred Downs by Jacqueline Downs

Tuesday, 13 February 1979

So, this is how it would have gone down. He'd have been sitting in his armchair, the one directly facing the telly. I'd have sat my ten-year-old self on his lap, or maybe on the pouffé (that's what we called it in the 1970s) in front of him. He'd have given me a ten-pence piece from his pocket, and I'd have told him about my day. I didn't talk to him for the money; I talked to him because we both loved having a chat between the end of teatime and my bedtime. But the money came in handy.

I can't remember what we spoke about that night. Maybe we discussed the excitement of the next day – his and my mum's twentieth wedding anniversary. I know *I* was excited about it. I'd been saving those ten-pence pieces and had used ten of them to buy a china bell from the local market. It was wrapped and hidden in my wardrobe and the next day he was going to see it.

Except he didn't.

Because on his way home from work he suffered two heart attacks. The ambulance crew brought him round after the first one, but his heart wore out. The second heart attack killed him.

Wednesday, 14 February 1979

I remember a lot about this evening from so very long ago. I remember us having our tea without him. I remember standing the china bell on the table with the anniversary card around it. I remember what I watched on TV while I waited for him to come home. I remember my mum going to the front door at regular intervals. I remember opening the door to the police officers. I remember saying to my mum, 'He never saw the present I bought him.'

That china bell.

Way back when

He was fifty-nine when he died. I was ten. That's quite an age gap. He was older than most of my friends' dads, but there were reasons for that. We were his second family. He'd been through this before.

There are things about my dad that I never found out about until long after his death, things that made me think, quite simply: My poor dad.

This is how it went down . . .

When he was thirteen, he came home from school and found his mum, dead, in a pool of her own blood. My own mum told me this story when I was in my thirties. For obvious reasons it wasn't something my dad ever spoke about to me. I was too young, and maybe even if he'd lived it wouldn't

184

have been something he wanted to dwell on. Somehow, somehow he managed to live with what had happened, what he had seen. He managed to go about his life, to form relationships.

One of those relationships was with the woman who became his first wife. They had a son. When their boy was a toddler she left, with my dad's best friend but without the son. Somehow my dad managed to live with this, managed to bring up his boy, managed to go about his life, to form other relationships.

He met my mum, had another son, then me. And then he went to work one day and he never came back.

His life was one that was built around people not coming back. It could have made him closed and wary. But he found a way to make it not matter. Maybe those losses made him crave company and family. I'm glad they did, because it meant for ten years I had a dad who took me to the park, to the seaside, to the fair, who built sandcastles with me, who watched me bounce and soar on trampolines embedded in south-coast beaches, who read to me, who talked to me every night before I went to bed.

And so when I think about what he went through, how he suffered, what he lost, and what he was emotionally brave enough to look for again, I no longer think, My poor dad. I think, My amazing, open, fantastic, optimistic dad. And I feel so very sad that I never got the chance to say this to him, because it's not the kind of credit he would ever have given himself.

Jacqueline Downs lives in Crystal Palace, where she is a writer and an editor.

I SAID TO MY MUM,
'WHO'S DAD?'

Anthony Monaghan & Roger McGough
by Nathan McGough

I had two fathers rather than one. I suppose it's not uncommon nowadays, but it wasn't typical when I was a child. I was born in Liverpool in 1960, in Knotty Ash, where Ken Dodd's Diddy Men come from, where the Jam Butty Mines are.

My parents were married very young. My dad was eighteen and my mum was just seventeen, eighteen by the time she had me. They were kids. My parents were from working-class families. My dad had refused National Service so he'd been conscripted to work in the coal mines instead. I guess they were happily married for a year and a half, but they were too young and they wanted totally different lives. My mum had a very artistic bent and she got offered a place at Liverpool Art School to do textiles and design when she was nineteen, but my dad was just a very traditional working-class man with, I suppose, all the prejudices that you might associate with that.

He thought men worked and women stayed at home, which didn't sit well with my mum at all. Although her family were very poor, she always had a desire to better herself. She left my dad when I was eighteen months old.

It was very uncommon to be a single parent in 1961, in Liverpool, but my mum decided that's what she'd be. My mother used to take me everywhere with her. She couldn't afford any childcare, so I was always down the art school with her, messing around, surrounded by art. I'd still see my dad on Saturdays, meeting him by the large clock in Central Station. At one o'clock there'd be a handover and he'd take me up to his parents' house in Knotty Ash, but my dad liked drinking and going to the bookie's. I have very strong childhood memories, and what I remember is being very, very bored at the weekend. He'd drop me off with his parents and then just go down the bookie's.

The most vivid memory I have of my real dad is him bringing me home to my mum's when I was three, back to Princess Avenue, Liverpool 8. We got off the bus and it started raining, so we ran. We were laughing and running through the rain. We got back to the house drenched and my mother went absolutely nuts, kicking off at him: 'Right, you're not going to see him any more, bringing him home soaking wet.' She was just looking for an excuse. I remember my dad pleading with her, saying, 'He's my son. I love him. Please don't stop me seeing him.' I can recall that moment when he left and just feeling incredibly sad because he was my father and I had this deep compassion for him. But I was so little that I was powerless to intervene. I couldn't articulate it. She'd decided it was inconvenient for her, but he was my dad. He wasn't hers. So if anybody was to say that I wasn't to see him any more then it should've been me. But I didn't have that intention, even though the Saturdays were boring.

I didn't see him again after that. I got a card on my sixth birthday that said, 'Happy Birthday, Love Dad.' I said to my mum, 'Who's Dad?' I was really confused. Children just live in the moment and three or four years is an eternity. By the time I'd got to five I'd totally forgotten I had a dad.

When I was six, my mother met a geography teacher who had aspirations to be a poet. He was called Roger McGough and they fell in love. They had this incredibly intense love affair, which Roger immortalised in *Summer with Monika*, his first published work. It's a wonderful piece of pop prose that I would read a lot as a kid. Monika was the name of the boutique my mother owned.

Roger came to live with us and I liked him. I remember the day he moved in. He'd been around quite a lot, which was fine. Then one day she said to me, 'When Roger comes around tonight I want you to say, "Hi Dad."' I was, like, why? 'Well, Roger's going to come live with us and it'll be funny.'

'I don't think it's funny. I don't want to do it.'

'Yeah, you do.' She basically made me. I obliged, because children do, and I laughed and he laughed, and from that point on I just called him Dad. And he was my dad.

He was a fun guy. He'd organise happenings underneath the Everyman bistro. He put on poetry nights. He'd write sketches, which Paul McCartney's brother, Mike, and John Gorman would perform with him. Then they formed their own performing group called the Scaffold and they'd do songs and poetry sketches. It proved to be very popular, so much so that they were signed to Decca Records and managed by Brian Epstein. They had a huge number-one hit for six weeks called 'Lily the Pink' in 1968.

He was a kind man and a good father, too, but my mother would keep him at arm's length to a degree. Whenever he fought my corner, she'd pull out the old 'He's my child, don't tell me what to do' card. But it was a happy house and ultimately they married and had two more children, Fin and Tom, born when I was eleven and thirteen respectively. We lived in this massive house that he bought with the 'Lily The Pink' money, and we had a nice family life until I hit sixteen and their marriage broke up, unable to withstand him being away touring all the time.

What killed it was he was offered a poetry fellowship at Loughborough University, which meant he was away for at least one year, living in the halls of residence. This was soon after my youngest brother was born. So they'd had these two young kids, plus me, a teenager who was up for mischief, and I think she just felt abandoned. Roger moved down to London, went out drinking and wrote a lot of bitter-tears poetry about the break-up. He wrote this addendum to *Monika*, which was brutally sad.

What's interesting to me is that I could've had a very different life, if my parents had stayed together in Knotty Ash, from the one I've actually had. My mother made her own life. She became a fashion designer; she opened a boutique. Then she decided after the marriage to Roger broke up that she wanted to work in television. After ten years she rose up to become one of the top light-entertainment producers: she produced *Blind Date*, *Surprise Surprise* and all those Saturday early-evening hits.

Roger being my stepfather really opened a door for me into pop culture too. I got to stay at Paul McCartney's house in St John's Wood as a kid, come to London regularly to things. I got involved in Factory Records because Anthony Wilson was a fan of my dad's poetry and would come and knock on the door. I was a brash gobshite young kid and he took a shine to me.

I did see my dad again. You know how when you're young

you have a root around in your parents' stuff? I was having a root around in my mother's things when I was about thirteen and I found this box in which was my birth certificate. I was born with the name Nathan Monaghan, which was my father's family name, and my mother was Thelma Monaghan when I was a kid. And this birth certificate said my dad's name: Anthony Frederick Monaghan. Wow, I twigged: that's my dad. It made me very curious so I started asking my mum and she said she didn't know where he was. I said I'd like to have met him by the time I was twenty-one. It got parked there and wasn't mentioned again.

I was in Manchester during the week of my twenty-first birthday and my mum called me, saying I needed to come back to Liverpool. Why? 'Because your dad is coming to see you.' I was, like, why is Roger coming to see me? 'No, it's Anthony – your real dad.' She'd been in touch with him because I'd said I wanted to meet him by the time I was twenty-one and I was about to be twenty-one. I couldn't believe she hadn't asked me. We hadn't mentioned it for seven years. So I got his number and called him up. I said something corny, like, 'Hello, this is a voice from the past.' We had a nice chat so I told him I'd come back on Sunday afternoon. I'd get the coach back from Manchester because it stopped at a place called the Rocket in Knotty Ash. He said he'd be at the bus stop to meet me at three o'clock.

I was kind of excited. I wanted to see what he was like because I hadn't seen him since I was three. What kind of man had he become? I had no fear.

I got off the bus at the Rocket at three and there was nobody there to meet me. I waited for five minutes, ten minutes. Right, well, I'm not the sort of person to hang around so I took the address of where he was staying and went there. I knocked on the door and this red-haired sixteen-year-old kid appeared. I said, 'I'm Nathan,' and he turned out to be my cousin. I asked if my dad was there. He said they'd left ages ago to meet me. So I came in and waited with this kid.

Around about five, my father and my uncle, who I'd never met, came bowling in and were surprised to see me there. They asked me where I was because they were waiting at the Rocket for me. I said they couldn't have been because I was there. My dad said, 'Well, we were in the pub across the road and we kept looking out to see if you were there.' I felt furious. He hadn't seen me for eighteen years, yet they couldn't stay out of the pub for the brief moment we were meant to meet. I like a drink. Meet me, take me to the pub across the road, get on it. Fine by me. Looking out the windows is not good enough for me.

I stayed on. It wasn't worth doing my nut over. His four brothers turned up, then all the wives and cousins. This was great: I was going to meet this whole family I never knew of. But my dad took all the men and sat us around the table in the front parlour, making all the women stay in the kitchen. It was meant to be that the men talked first and the women and children talked later. I'm thinking, Woah. That's not how I was raised. All my friends in Liverpool were politicised and feminists, and I counted myself as one. I wasn't very comfortable with the man-to-man stuff. It didn't sit right.

Eventually I got to meet my uncle Paul's wife. It was her house, and she was lovely. She said we'd all go out to the social that evening, play bingo and have a great family night out. Amazing. My dad said he wanted to take me out first and have a one-to-one. 'By the way,' he said, 'here is a card for your twenty-first from your auntie Catherine. She can't be here and she's gutted.' There was a five-pound note in the card. Very nice.

We went for a walk and my dad said that it was important

I understand that he'd always wanted to see me. He said it was my mum who'd asked him to stay away. He'd kept all the letters they'd sent each other and he showed me the love letters, to prove that it was a genuine marriage. Then he showed me a letter that my mum had sent, saying every time I went to stay with him I had a really bad asthma attack so it was best that I don't see him any more. That was a lie. Then he pulled up his sleeve and he had my name tattooed on his arm. I felt for him. He'd carried this around his whole life.

We walked up to a pub and he asked if I could lend him the fiver that my auntie had given me. All right, fine. We had pints. It came to seven thirty and I told him we had to go back to meet everyone, but he wouldn't leave the boozer. 'I'll give you a bit of advice,' he said. 'Don't pay attention to what women tell you to do. Do what you want.' It's the worst advice you could ever give anyone.

He kept me in the pub until closing time. We eventually got back to the house bevvied and my auntie went off massively at him, but also at me. I just thought, This has not been a great day. It freaked me out. Sometimes you just can't fix what happened in the past, I decided. I thought I was glad that my mum left him and met Roger because, although it wasn't without its pain, it was also fabulous in many ways.

I never spoke to my birth dad again. About five years ago, though, I started thinking about my own daughters. I was estranged from my children's mother for a while. It was a bad break-up and I went through what my dad went through. It's incredibly painful when you cherish your children and you are denied seeing them. Their mother and I fixed that in the end. We're friends again and I have a great relationship with my kids. But I started to have a bit of empathy with my birth father. I thought, He must be an old guy now, in his seventies. I should

193

just find him, tell him he's got some grandchildren, ask him if he's okay for money and give him whatever he needs. I looked into it on the Internet and discovered very quickly that he'd died in 2007, at sixty-seven. I felt really gutted. He was gone.

Recently, I tracked down his death certificate and learnt he died in a nursing home of dementia. I've started to think about trying to get in touch with his family to find out more about him and more about his parents. There are so many questions I have that I can't ask, but I suppose that must be the case for most people when their parents die. I don't resent my mother leaving him and I'm grateful for the life we had with Roger. Their hard work inspired me greatly, inspired my brothers and sisters too. I have a lovely extended family. But I do think it's wrong for women to stop the fathers of their children from seeing them simply because it's not convenient any more. It's not their dad. It's the kid's dad. You don't get that time again.

Nathan McGough has been managing bands such as Happy Mondays, Shack and White Lies since the 1980s.

AS OF THIS AFTERNOON, HE WAS AT HOME IN THE GARDEN

Allan Edward Burgess by Tim Burgess

There's a dadness that all dads share. I debuted in the job only fifteen months ago and my dadisms are on the increase: a son helps you shape your own fatherhood but also lights up the past and casts your own dad in a slightly different view. I remembered shared moments, like me learning to swim in Eccles baths; sitting beside him as he rowed a boat on a lake when I was six; watching Pearson, Coppell and the Greenhoffs taking on the hirsute might of the old first division together; caravan holidays – Skegness once and North Wales the rest of the time. By the 1980s we'd upgraded to camping trips in France.

The 1970s were not easy for dads – times could be tough and it was all bottled-up emotions, Blue Stratos and driving gloves. Back then paternity leave was unheard of; bonding with your children involved holding them awkwardly while the new mum wrestled with a Vesta curry for tea.

I saved up and bought a Triumph Dolomite and, although I'd never taken any interest or offered any help while my dad spent time maintaining and cleaning the family car, he and I would spend hours working on my car. I was chief passer of tools and carrier of stuff and he would deftly change the oil, the gearbox or carry out any number of jobs that I'd not know where to start on. He never complained and it's where we'd swap news, grumble about the female side of the family and I'd learn about his life and he about mine.

The story of me and my dad contains little drama. I was never chucked out, beaten up, and as of this afternoon, he was at home in the garden. The longer the story goes on, the more I appreciate him for the man he is. He was a keen sportsman and played rugby for Salford and Sedgley Park; he was a season-ticket holder at Manchester United from when he first saw them in 1956 until about six years ago when the actions of the American owners meant he stopped going. He was a draughtsman at ICI, so he's always had an eye for order and detail, but he was patient with me when I lacked both growing up.

In 1996 I was invited to Manchester United as one of only 150 guests to a new restaurant that was opening. Ryan Giggs and Gary Neville were fans of my band the Charlatans so I was asked along with a guest. I took my dad and he met some of the legends he'd watched play over the previous thirty years, as well a new lad, David Beckham, who came over to say hi. My dad was never big on special treatment, presents and the like, but that evening I could tell he was glad the band had done so well as to secure him an invitation.

One of the only jobs I had before I joined the Charlatans was sorting and delivering the post on the site where he worked. He was held in such high esteem I didn't make a noise about the fact he was my dad for fear I might seem a little less rebellious. But I idolised him for who he was and how people viewed him. My interest in music had been with me from a young age and was all-consuming. In my early teens, though, I harboured some sort of misplaced desire to follow in his footsteps and become a draughtsman. You had to be good at maths, and I wasn't. I remember taking my borderline-fail exam slip home and went to find my dad. He was sweeping up. I made him a cup of tea and muttered about my grade while he was turned the other way. I thought he might fly off the handle, but he stayed perfectly calm, carried on sweeping the floor and said, 'Tim, please don't try to be a draughtsman – I don't think it's very you.' I took that moment to be the green light to keep up my interest in being a singer in a band. I've never checked with him, but it was a big moment for me.

He had his garage, still does. Always a job on the go. Painting stuff, bleeding radiators, mowing, drilling and sawing till it got dark. When I was very small he used to heat up the Meccano steam engine he'd built. It made a whistling noise that we both waited for eagerly, and then the wheels would go round fast and I thought it was the best thing ever. Well, that lived in the garage. I've been in there with my boy, Morgan, and can see myself standing there a lifetime ago.

He made me cry when he read out the eulogy for my granddad. Dad is the eldest son out of three and I'd never seen him so stoic. He made a remarkable speech about dads and how valued his was. It was touching and so emotional. It really gave me a sense of how he felt. The love for my dad is just beyond words – and to see him with my son gives my world the most amazing symmetry.

So, that's my dad, no drama, no outbursts, always welcoming of my friends and as solid as a rock for me and my life, which sometimes seemed as if I was lost to the world. Never judging, always there and so easy to idolise. That's my dad.

Tim Burgess is the singer with the Charlatans, among other things.

YEARS FROM NOW, A CHAIN OF IRRESISTIBLE GENETIC CODE WILL SPARK UP

Michael Segal by Victoria Segal

There is one thing, more than anything else, I suspect my father wants me to say about him. He would never admit it directly, but he says it about his dad, and I think I can see him watching to make sure I've taken note, filed it away for later use. It's not an original thought – the general consensus is that it's from Mark Twain – and my father's version is a paraphrase, but its appeal is clear: 'When I was young, I used to think my father knew nothing. As I got older, I was amazed at how much the old man had learned.'

Unless it turns out that he's been working undercover as a neurosurgeon, I've always found it difficult to imagine a situation that would demand those words. More likely I'll suddenly announce, 'I'd love to go and see some motor racing' or 'The time in my life has come when I must learn about eighteenth-century naval history' – both of which would doubtless be welcome, if not quite as good. It's not that I think he knows nothing. He was a hairdresser on a South American cruise ship in the sixties, a job description that, on paper, makes my existence seem faintly improbable. It was a billet that left him with a Polari-enriched vocabulary, a killer collection of bossa-nova records and a rainbow parrot called Robert. I'd quite like to know what happened to Robert, sold on before my parents got married, but any new information on the bird's whereabouts, while interesting, wouldn't really warrant the Twain quote.

When my dad says it about his father, it's still perplexing to me: my late grandfather knew a lot about pickling and hosiery, but that can't be what he means. Instead, it comes over as a comforting tidying up, neat myth-making, smoothing away the edges and irritations that came with his real-life dad: the trail of red and white betting-shop pens, extra salt added to already heavily salted food, a market stall that required a son to run it in the holidays. When your make-up includes the East End plus Eastern Europe, the pull towards sentimentality is strong – not so much the strain that involves weeping tears of gin over adorable urchins, but the one that calls for a wistful far-off gaze, a tremulous pause, biting back emotion as, somewhere, a violin wails.

My suspicion, then, is that one day I will say it. A few years from now, a chain of irresistible genetic code will spark up and I'll suddenly look away, and sigh, and say to my children, 'When I was young, I used to think my father knew nothing. As I got older, I was amazed at how much the old man had learned.' Sentimental idiot, they'll think, rolling their eyes, but lost in violins and the distant, reassuring squawk of parrots, I won't notice.

Victoria Segal writes about music, television and books from London's filthiest desk.

THE THINGS WE DO AND SAY AS PARENTS HAVE CONSEQUENCES

My father by Shami Chakrabarti

Children listen to the most unlikely things. There are events we remember from childhood, lessons learned from our parents that were never intended as anything more than passing remarks. It was a moment like this that set me on a journey that ultimately led me to Liberty – and I have my father to thank for it.

As an eleven-year-old girl watching the TV news in my parents' north-west London semi, I remember being transfixed by the seemingly endless updates in the hunt for the Yorkshire Ripper. One evening, unnerved by the coverage, I said something about what they should do to 'this animal' or 'monster', or something along those lines, when he was caught. In my dad's first and perhaps last Atticus Finch moment, he asked me to consider that no justice system capable of human design or operation can ever be perfect. What would it feel like, I remember him saying, to be the one wrongly convicted person in a thousand or a million walking to the gallows or electric chair or lethal injection? What would it feel like when every due-process appeal was exhausted and when even your own family no longer believed you – yet you went to your death knowing that you hadn't done the terrible thing for which you were about to be executed?

That evening my father's words captured my imagination and turned my stomach – it makes the hairs on my neck stand up as I write. I duly reconsidered and never looked back. If I went on in adult life to become the bugbear of so many authoritarian men, they have only one of their own number – my dear old dad – to blame.

Decades later, my father read this story in a magazine interview I'd done. I was worried he thought I'd compromised his privacy in some way by recounting it. In fact he said he couldn't remember the incident at all. He was, until recently, unaware of the great influence he'd had on this central part of my life.

The things we say and do as parents have consequences, for good and ill. Growing up, another father had a huge impact on me – Atticus Finch, in *To Kill a Mockingbird*. Working for Liberty, I've often thought back to Atticus's advice to his daughter: 'No matter what anybody says to you, don't you let 'em get your goat. Try fighting with your head for a change.'

So, imagine my excitement at the publishing event of 2015 when Harper Lee's *Go Set a Watchman* was unleashed. Imagine my anguish as our childhood heroine Scout grows up and Atticus grows old and falls from grace. The Atticus of *Watchman* has either grown cynical or afraid at the pace of progressive change and race equality, or his human-rights values were always locked in a courtroom, like some people's religion remains in church. The shift in attitude of the older advocate breaks his daughter's heart – and, no doubt, those of thousands of readers.

Thankfully, Jean Louise had already absorbed the wisdom of the younger Atticus, and it was those early lessons that stuck. But our fathers are human. They disappoint us – whether through a thoughtless snide comment, or the repetition of poisonous ideologies.

Who knows where I might have ended up had my father not challenged my apparent fervour for the death penalty? The moment might have faded from my memory, or I could have found myself fighting alongside those I now seek to stand against.

As it happens, I feel lucky the lesson stuck.

Shami Chakrabarti is director of Liberty, the civil-liberties advocacy organisation.

WE WERE LIKE BROTHERS

Dave Hawley by Richard Hawley

My dad was four years old when his own dad took him to the cinema to see *Zorro*. Dad fell asleep during the film, and when he woke up, his dad wasn't there. He'd been abandoned. Eventually he was reunited with his mother, my grandmother, Audrey, but the experience really fucked him up.

It was the late forties, early fifties, in Sheffield, and my parents were dead poor. Divorce was a social no-no for their kind then, so my dad was farmed out to his cousins, partly in Portsmouth and partly in Bishop Auckland. When he was a teenager he came back to Sheffield and was brought up in Parsons Cross, which was a no-nonsense place.

My dad was into two things above all else: music and motorbikes. He was a biker all his life, until the mid-seventies when he came off one on the way to get some fish and chips, waking up underneath Wicker Arches with a dog licking the blood from his face. My mum said enough was enough after that and he had to knock it on the head.

It was his love of bikes that helped turn him on to rock 'n' roll. He had a job as a dispatch rider in the fifties. He was in a bikers' caff in the New Forest when 'My Baby Left Me' by Elvis came on the jukebox and that was it. It blew his mind. It's hard to imagine now when everything is there at the touch of a button, but you had to work hard at an obsession in those days. He told me this story about getting an American pen pal through an offer on the back of a Kellogg's Corn Flakes pack when he was a teenager. This pen pal sent him Ray Charles's 'What I Say', the original single on Atlantic Records, which made him the coolest guy in England.

He was always way ahead of the curve, musically. There was a record shop that he used to go to in Sheffield called Violet May's, which was an incredible place. Violet had connections to the Liverpool dockers and she would get all the records that nobody else could get. My dad heard everything first because he'd hang around there obsessively.

He had a damn good shot at being a professional musician himself. He played guitar with Sonny Boy Williamson, Memphis Slim; he went on tour with Bill Monroe. And he was in a trio called the Lorne Gibson Trio, who nearly made it. He was in bands from when he was really young. He was in a band with my mum and auntie called the Whirlwinds. They were on a talent show on the BBC in Manchester in 1961 and they came second. The winners were the Beatles. He was so close so often.

Music was his all-encompassing passion, but it became a darkness for him. There's a temptation to get to a certain point in your life and then walk towards your death backwards. I think Dad did a bit of that. 'What if' and 'if only'. It was so much harder to make it as a musician in the early sixties, though he gave it a right good go.

My mum had fallen in love with him when they were doing

an audition for some band or other in a cinema in Sheffield. She said he looked like the most dangerous, dirty biker that she'd ever seen. He was wearing a drape, he had a massive quiff and had these filthy jeans on, and then he got up on stage and sang a Gene Vincent song and, bang, she was in love. Exactly what you shouldn't go for, she said, but she couldn't help it.

They were fifteen or sixteen when they got together and they got divorced during the steel strikes of the 1980s. There's that old cliché 'Money goes out the door and love's not far behind.' I don't think it was actually money that did for them, more the endless stress of working at the steelworks. My dad was a union leader and the stress of it all just raked up the memories of his childhood. He ended up having a massive nervous breakdown. It was bad at the time but eventually it was happily ever after. My mum remarried, they're still together, and my dad had a partner too, Frida. I think he found some genuine spiritual happiness in that relationship, though he became a bit of a hermit in his later years. He never had any help with his abandonment issues, which I never really understood as a kid. I wish I had. I think it coloured his whole life.

I paint a dark picture of him but our relationship was very close, very deep, unusually so, and he was a truly great dad. We were like brothers. The thing that bonded us was always music. I remember we'd go record shopping together, to Kenny's Records on the Wicker. It was a rock 'n' roll-blues-country-rockabilly place. I discovered so much there with him. Dad had over a thousand albums, all these amazing 45s, and that's what shaped me. Music bonded us, as did politics. Literature, too. In fact, the only thing that I am ashamed of with my dad is this . . .

You get to a point in your teenage years where you stretch the envelope so far that you're almost baiting your parents. I was in the fifth year, about to go to sixth form, at a working-class school in Sheffield, but it filled me with a sense of curiosity and awe. I was taking in everything to do with music, art, literature. I was a sponge. I was also being a smart-arse, a show-off, and coming home with these books by Kafka, Kerouac, Wilfred Owen, Sartre and so forth, waving them around in front of my parents as if I'd invented reading. I always had a paperback in my pocket.

My dad once asked me what I was reading and I said, 'Why would you be interested in this? You're just a thick steelworker.' I can't believe to this day that those words came out of my mouth. My granddad was sitting with him at the kitchen table, and that they didn't give me the good hiding I deserved proves what great men they were. They just said, 'Oh, aye. We'll leave it to you, then.' I carried on like this for a few weeks, baiting my dad with my books, until the day he came back from work on a Friday night and I was sitting on the end of his bed playing my guitar. I had worked out the ending to 'Lawdy Miss Clawdy' by Elvis and I was very pleased with myself. My dad, meanwhile, had done a fourteen-hour shift and was taking Mum out for a piss-up. He was getting ready, putting a shirt on in his room as I played the guitar and he said to me, 'Oh, I meant to show you something. It's about those books you've been reading.' I knew I'd been a dick and he knew I'd been a dick, but he hadn't said anything because he was too cool.

Anyway, he parted his shirts and jackets in their horrible MFI wardrobe and said, 'Have a look, son, when I'm gone, it might be of interest to you.' Jacket on, comb and fags in pocket, off he went with my mother for the night.

When they'd gone I looked in the wardrobe. There was every book that I'd come home with and loads more. He'd been there before me. He'd read all those books that I'd rubbed his nose in and so many more. I sat there and I wept. I was

214

so ashamed. I realised what a great man he was for not taking me to task, showing me up. From that point on, my gob was zipped. I just had to learn from the master.

I think very subtly he showed me how to be a man. I lost my virginity when I was fourteen and I had to talk to my dad about it because it freaked me out. All he said was 'Well, it's gonna happen, kid.' That just gave me perspective. He did the same when I was heavily addicted to drugs. I was not in a good place. I was touring a lot but I wasn't really sure where the fuck I was going and I was already a father, had been since I was twenty-six. It was only when I became thirty that the penny dropped that this was not a good look. I had a thirtieth party in a pub. My dad came and gave me a card. I didn't open it until the next day with a colossal hangover and then pissed myself laughing because it said, 'Happy birthday son. 30? I never thought you'd make it to Thursday!' He was a funny fucker, but he could see what I was doing too. Then I got the call from Jarvis Cocker to play with Pulp that saved my hide.

Dad always had an hour for me, even when he was fucked. He'd work twelve-hour days, then play in bands at night. But he always fitted time in for me. He'd come home and eat the biggest meal you've ever seen – one of those Christmas platters that you get, he'd have one every night when he was working, piled high. He'd eat the lot even though he was dead wiry, then he'd go play with bands, come home at one in the morning after a skinful, go to bed, then get up for work at six. Just such a hard man, but also gentle and kind. Hilarious, too.

Even though I surpassed what he achieved musically, he never resented me. We had a great relationship up until the end. The last words he said to me on his death-bed, before he slipped away into a coma, were 'I love you, son.' Like a lot of men and women from that generation and that class, and geographically here in Sheffield, they made the best of what they'd been given. They weren't worried about having two holidays a year, or their bonus, or their new Xbox. They were looking out for each other, hoping that everyone got paid enough every week to put food on their tables. As a community, those steel workers really were a different class. I can't fault them. I aspire to be them. And my dad was the very pinnacle. He was a first-wave biker Teddy Boy and he played rock 'n' roll. He taught me to stand up on my own two feet. What's not to love? I miss him so much.

Richard Hawley is a singer and musician who has released seven albums under his own name. He lives in Sheffield with his wife and children.

I DO NOT KNOW THIS OLD MAN

Goodbye by Lubi Barre

The man staring at me through my iPhone screen is old. His hair is completely grey and close-cropped. He's lethargic, his eyes heavy, his voice slow. He used to know several languages but now can barely speak his native tongue. A tongue he had passed on to me but that I barely use in my new life.

I say, 'Father, it's your daughter Lubna.'

He hardly responds, looking back with low lids at the iPad shoved in his face. My mother goads him to respond and, like a good schoolboy, he says, 'Hello, how are you doing?' rehearsed.

I say, 'Father, it's Axado,' and suddenly he bursts into a knowing smile, remembering the special nickname he gave me as a child: *Sunday*. I say, 'Father, it's Axado, look at my baby son, we say hello.' His smile widens, his soul remembering his love for babies even if his brain can't comprehend that this one belongs to me.

I do not know this old man. The father I knew and left four years ago was old only in years. His voice was strong, leaving me pleading messages to return his calls as I erased them.

And now I find myself picking up my son, like a prop, and presenting him to his grandfather on a phone screen. They both look at each other, like strangers, unaware they share twenty-five per cent genetically.

I am not sure if they will get the chance to meet. I know for sure that my father can no longer give me advice, does not have the strength to hold his grandson, to make the connections needed. I know that he will not be able to change my son's diaper when his own needs changing.

I wished it did not take me this long to become responsible, to understand how *fixable* everything is. I wished I knew the fragility of life before the feel of my son's new skin.

I say 'Goodbye, Father,' and wave my son's hands for him while his own lies limp. My mother prompts him to answer and he says, like an old man, 'Goodbye, have a nice day.'

Lubi Barre is a writer living in Hamburg, Germany, with her husband and two children.

HE WAS THE SORT OF MAN WHO WORE A TIE TO MOW THE LAWN

Derek Mulvey by John Mulvey

On the train to work the other day, I read a review of the new novel by an American author, David Gilbert, I hadn't come across before. The book is called *& Sons*, and James Wood's essay focuses on one of Gilbert's main themes: the 'emotional reticence' displayed by men of a certain age. 'More open, more voluble children must become expert readers of patriarchal gaps and silences,' writes Wood, 'in order to make sense of what [Gilbert] finely calls "these heavily redacted men".'

'Heavily redacted men': it's a resonant phrase. My father was not, I would guess, an exact match for Gilbert's protagonist, but he was innately discreet, to a degree many of us would now consider pathological. Even the mechanics of writing about him seem absurd, not least because he lived in a world without the Internet, where keyboards were restricted to typing pools, and a computer filled an entire room in the town-hall basement. But it would be the disclosures here, not the technicalities, that he would find most incomprehensible.

We frequently assume that men like my father, born in 1929 and brought up through the war in what I suspect were fairly straitened circumstances, were hiding something. In reality, I think a lot of them merely lacked the specific vocabulary, or the sense of entitlement, to express themselves. To reveal his beliefs – my father took the impartiality of his job in local government so seriously, he wouldn't even tell my mother how he voted – would be an unimaginable dereliction of duty. To talk about the past – the financial imperatives that meant he had to abandon his part-time studies in law to look after his parents, his fleeting career as a jazz drummer during National Service – would be a betrayal of stoic codes; codes so embedded in his make-up that he had no idea he was following them.

All this redaction must make him seem emotionally constrained, but he wasn't really like that at all. He was engaged, affectionate and always supportive. He was a figure of fundamental constancy, rooted in the consolations of family, and thinking of him makes me wonder, as I over-intellectualise and over-analyse so much from day to day (and, yes, I'm doing it now), how different an unexamined life might be. We routinely think of people without an accessible hinterland to be either deceitful or boring, perhaps even impoverished. I wonder, instead, if they show us something else – that contentment is possible.

It would be disingenuous to pretend that my father's life was entirely untroubled. He clearly worried about and brooded over his work; during one of those periodic upheavals of local government, his hair turned white more or less overnight, and most of his eyebrows fell out from what I can only assume now was the stress of the situation. Perhaps, if he could have openly countenanced the actual concept of stress, those who loved him might have been able to help him through it.

But that was not how my dad functioned. He was indulgent to me whenever I was sick, and doted on my mother, but for his own part he believed that illness was mostly psychosomatic. As what he would see as a consequence, he never really seemed to be ill. Later on, he evidently decided – keeping his own counsel on the subject, of course – that this would be the best way to deal with the onset of Alzheimer's disease.

It's not easy to chart with much certainty how long my father suffered because, for a good few years, he was so adept at masking it. If he carried on doing the *Daily Mail* crossword, kept acing the tests set by the doctors, and staunchly refused to acknowledge there was anything wrong with him, then surely he could fend off even the most debilitating of conditions. If he could beat a cold by denying its existence, then maybe he could do the same to Alzheimer's. He was a quiet and amiable man, happiest on the periphery of social gatherings, and it wasn't always obvious that he was becoming quieter, a little more placid, a little more detached from what was going on around him.

Gradually, though, the strain of maintaining his dignity in public meant that, alone with my mother, he became overwhelmed by confusion and paranoia while never, in his moments of lucidity, allowing himself to talk about what was happening. He hallucinated people moving around the house. He obsessed over financial minutiae, and became convinced that my mother was involved in nefarious plots against him. He rarely slept, and so my mum, who cared for him twenty-four hours a day, rarely slept either.

Alzheimer's stories feel painfully idiosyncratic when you're living through them, but many follow an uncannily predictable trajectory. In the winter of 2008, my mother slipped on some ice and was injured just badly enough that she could not, for what was expected to be a few days or so, look after my father. He was taken into an NHS care home, where his condition abruptly degenerated. With the divide between public life and home life removed, his attempts to repress the disease took on a desperate new intensity.

Soon after Christmas, my father barricaded himself into his room on several occasions, and was removed to a hospital psychiatric ward, where his condition was eventually stabilised. He had, though, been defeated: he could not do anything for himself now, in fact could barely talk, and seemed, at last, benignly accepting of his situation.

For the last few months of my dad's life, he lived in an absolute shithole of a private nursing home because it was the only place in my home town that accepted patients with severe dementia. The purported benefits of private healthcare are that competition forces up standards, but in a small north Midlands town that can only sustain one Alzheimer's facility, such standards can be blithely ignored in the pursuit of profit. My father spent his final days in a place where no one had bothered to wash the bloodstains out of the curtains; where farcically underpaid, undertrained and unmotivated staff blasted Radio 1 at octogenarians as they were spoon-fed dinner; where the windows overlooked a river, and a small lake, but were set so high in the walls that the residents could not see out of them from a seated position. My mother and I were horrified and powerless; my father seemed calmly oblivious – though, not for the first time, it may have been a mistake to try to second-guess what was going on in his head.

A collateral cruelty of Alzheimer's disease is the way it robs family and friends of their memories. By the time he died in

June 2009 – a few days after his eightieth birthday, three months after the birth of my second son – it had been so long since my father was entirely himself, it was hard to remember what he used to be like. For his funeral, I tried to piece together some thoughts and, though I hope I wasn't quite deluded enough to propose canonisation, I said something about how he never gossiped or sniped at people; how he never seemed to be envious, or bitter, or vindictive.

He could be irritated by trivialities, but his deeper tolerance of my moods and choices seems, with hindsight, to be verging on the superhuman (I write now, transparently, as a father), even when those choices must have been bewildering to him. He never complained that his only child, the first in the family to go to university, couldn't be bothered to endure a graduation ceremony that would have publicly validated his pride. He never told me to cut my hair when I let it grow untamed for years, though he was the sort of man who wore a tie to mow the lawn.

I didn't realise what I was learning at the time, but he taught me some inspiring things; by implication and consistency, not by didacticism. Cricket, he intimated, is a wonderful game, but it's hardly a tragedy when Nottinghamshire lose. You can play records by the Fall all you want, but one day you might grasp that Duke Ellington is pretty good, too. And unstinting love can be a vital presence in your life, even if it cannot always be articulated.

John Mulvey is the editor of *Uncut* magazine.

I FOLLOW MY FATHER

My Old Man by Tilda Swinton

I follow my father.

I follow my father as he makes his way down the greenhouse, delicately tottering forward, swaying slightly back, swinging his hip sideways, then plunging onward, as if to a deep beat. As a disco move, it's pretty slick, insouciant, even. As a mode of reliable perambulation, it is a feat of keen nerve.

My father was once a contender for the four-minute mile. Then he went to his war at nineteen and was wounded sharpish. Being prepped for an MRI scan last year, the routine question about any bits of metal in him jogged his memory for the first time in 70 years: he remembered hazily hearing a doctor bent over him in a field station mumbling something about leaving the bullet where it was in his thigh so as not to cause any more fuss. Within a month, similarly dedicated to fuss-lessness, making his way back across Germany to his regiment, he was shot off a tank and lay for twenty-four hours before being found a second time. With a robust sense of family tradition, his own father having lost his left foot in the trenches in 1917, he lost his left leg at this point.

I follow my father as his stairlift creeps him up the stairs. His dog tucks under his knees on the footrest for the journey, citing the same special privileges as those faithful companions immortalised under the heels of mossy stone knights on their perpetual backs under chestnut trees or vaulted ceilings.

My father said little to me during my childhood, although I know that by the time I was twelve he considered me 'contrary'. He used this word many times with definite emphasis, as if that were the end of it, like he was nailing a banner above my head, or an archivist's stamp. Looking back, I like to wonder now if it wasn't a word chosen and meted out with a sense of savoured satisfaction. Although, to be honest, I fully doubt it.

When I was eight, I sat on the floor by the fire, leaning my back against his armchair. He reached down, as he read his paper and absentmindedly twiddled my ear. I had a small winter rip in the seam of the lobe: as he twisted, a trickle of blood made its way down my neck. I could not speak for the confusions of pain and the incredulous delight that he was showing me – however distractedly, however much he had clearly mistaken me for a spaniel – this affection, this physical familiarity and ownership.

I follow my father's buggy with its bouncy cavalier caterpillar tread over the tree roots and around rhododendron dens as he parlays a running commentary on the particulars of the glories of the May garden wood. I surreptitiously film the back of his head, his conducting arm with its knotted knuckle-end. I am careful not to be caught capturing.

When I was ten, swinging on the back of my dining room chair one Sunday lunchtime, having told me to desist three times, he turned like a twist of lightning and fetched me a spank with the flat blade of the carving knife with such force and precision that there was a pink strip on the thigh south of my summer shorts for a week – and I lost my appetite for roast chicken for a good while longer.

My father has soup for lunch every day except Sunday, now. Soup and melba toast. I have been trying to source double handled soup cups – boullion bowls? – for months. There is now only one left with both ears standing. Does nobody want to drink their soup two-handed any more?

My mother died on a Wednesday morning three years ago in her morphine-powered bed in the drawing room just as he was down the other end of the polished corridor starting on his breakfast. I had opened the curtains after that final night with her: the long labour of her dying was about to fold itself up. When it did, the blessed peace was everywhere.

My father, having been brought to see her, sat alone for a few seconds with his beloved-beyond-all-on-earth for fifty-eight years. I watched him through the interior window as he fished his massive handkerchief out of his pocket and powdered his cheek with it.

When he left the room, his first words, to my brother coming towards him were, memorably 'Well, your recce to the crematorium yesterday was not in vain'.

Equally memorably, when we sat round the dining room table an hour later with the undertaker, discussing a date for the funeral, he declared 'Well, my diary for next week is entirely blank'.

As children, my brothers and I dreaded nothing quite as much as a solo drive with my father. His ability to say precisely not one thing to us during an entire journey of several hours was breathtaking.

One day, he lobbed over the top of his paper 'Treasure Island!', as my brothers and I struggled with a crossword clue. It was the only time he ever participated in this daily pre-lunch ritual of our school holidays – and the solution was right. Last month, watching University Challenge with my children, he called out the same answer – 'Treasure Island!' – after forty years: different programme, bingo again. Double bullseye, however widely spaced.

My father loves Nana Mouskouri. He loves regimental band music. And Morecambe and Wise. And trees. He wears exquisitely jewel-coloured cardigans with their elbows frayed like exotic lilies. He is as handsome and upright as a pale tribal shield. He is grand and childlike, transcendent and lost, in equal measure. He is 90 now. I bring him his favourite chocolate raisins and hide them in a wooden box by his chair. We never refer to this supply. Its reliability has become part of our shared ideology, my old man and me.

Tilda Swinton lives in the Highlands of Scotland. She makes films, has three brothers and is the mother of twins.

A LITTLE KID DOESN'T
FORGET THAT

Joseph Kessler by Felix Kessler

'Happy families are all alike,' is how *Anna Karenina* begins.
'Every unhappy family is unhappy in its own way.'

Who am I to argue with Leo Tolstoy? His parents died when
he was young; his life was long, turbulent, and often unhappy.
He also wrote *War and Peace* among other light classics.

As for me, even the name Felix means happy, as my parents
told me. Thanks to them, I've been not only happy but lucky.

Born in Vienna, I wasn't yet five when German tanks rolled
into Austria and cheering crowds greeted them. Our neighbours cheered, too, when guys (Germans or Austrians) wearing
Nazi armbands marched down our street. A little kid doesn't
forget that.

Soon after the Anschluss, Germany's annexation of Austria
in 1938, my mother began schlepping me from office to office
trying to get a 'visa'. What was a visa? Why did we need it?
How I hated that word. 'Visa' sounded like 'vaccine', though

in a way I guess it was: it inoculated us against Nazism, the disease that infected Austria and soon most of Europe.

I couldn't understand this visa business; we kept going to these dusty offices where people were nasty and rude to my wonderful mother. After one such bad morning, we came home empty-handed to find Grandfather sitting by the window reading his newspaper. Suddenly there were shouts from our courtyard. Were those men in armbands now downstairs about to throw rocks through our window?

My mother rushed us into a bathroom. She pleaded with Grandfather to come from the window, but he just sat there smoking and reading. She shook her head and began muttering to herself, something I had never seen her do before.

Okay, nothing happened. Grandfather David was still sitting there when we came out. But Mother's own family history hadn't prepared her for happy outcomes. Her father, like Hitler, was a corporal in Austria's army in the First World War. Unlike der Führer, Berthold Morgenstern was Jewish and was killed in that war. My mother hardly got to know him, and I not at all.

In the end, we did get those visas and left. So did my father's parents, three brothers, his sister and their families. And my grandmother (Mom's mother) came to live with us. None of us had to scrub sidewalks with toothbrushes, as did some Jews while smiling Nazi thugs watched and other Viennese stood idly by. Perhaps you've seen those pictures in history books. We were spared that, and far worse: the trains to Auschwitz and Dachau, the desperate attempts to escape the death camps. How did we avoid that when so many Jews didn't? How did my parents manage to flee when so many wealthy, better-educated Jews perished?

My wife Jair wondered how my father, a bookbinder, understood how urgent it was to get out of Austria. My son Daniel, at seven, also asked whether our neighbours wouldn't have helped or hidden us if they knew we were in danger. I asked about that, too, not long after we'd come and were happily settled in America.

'Ah, we knew them,' Dad said, meaning the Viennese. Does that sound like prejudice on his part? Seeing what ensued, no one could say we'd acted hastily. Immediately after the Anschluss, Jews were urged to leave. 'We didn't have to be told twice,' Dad said. He was prescient: no matter how hard Jews tried later, they couldn't escape from Austria.

The Nazis let us go after my parents paid various fees and taxes and gave up our home and bookbinding business. Six months after the Nazis entered Austria, we took an overnight train from Vienna and arrived in Switzerland on 19 September 1938, joining my cousins as temporary residents.

Five months later we sailed from Antwerp to America on the *Westernland*. A picture of my father on a deck-chair makes the eleven-day voyage seem more like a winter cruise than a ship filled with refugees, as its manifest shows.

We arrived on 15 February 1939, less than a year after Austria's annexation. My father was just thirty-two, younger than any of his grandsons today, and didn't look that old.

The US welcomed us once we found sponsors, a family of American Jews who vouched for us though they didn't know us. They were 'Uncle Joe' and 'Aunt Laura', lived in Jersey City, New Jersey, and so we settled there.

Dad changed his first name from Josef to Joseph and added a middle initial – J for Justus, he said – that the Nazis had stuck on his emigration papers, for Jude or Jew. It was his way of making the best of things.

He'd dreamt of becoming a lawyer. As a skilled bookbinder he found work soon after arriving and said it beat having to master a new legal system, again making the best of things. Still, he was fired from this job on his first day.

He was given written instructions to cut paper into 8 x 27-inch sheets. He'd misread it as 8 x 21; the seven didn't have the little dash Europeans used. Welcome to America.

Dad did get another job, and four years later (in 1943) he bought a failing bookbinder on 23rd Street in Manhattan. (In going through his papers later I saw it was named Foldwell; I like to think it was the same outfit that fired him.)

As his own boss, Dad was at work by 6.30 a.m. and rarely home before 7 p.m. Mother worked with him, as did five or six African-American women and Ludwig, a German refugee. It upset me when Dad yelled at Ludwig, who had a concentration-camp number on one muscular arm. Ludwig didn't seem bothered by Dad's temper.

After Mother was held up for the payroll one day, their lesson (to me) was never to argue with a gunman. They nixed my suggestion to use cheques because their workers preferred cash. Still, they now locked the door on paydays.

In 1944, a year before the war ended, we all became US citizens. I became a real American sooner, thanks both to school and the friends I'd made on our block – kids like Spanky Nelson, Hungry Dunnigan, the Galvin brothers, Frankie Fanelli, Ally Ahearn, Joey Schultz and Jimmy Day, my first and best friend. Not another Jewish boy on that block.

We played stoopball and stickball in summers, rode sleds down the street in winter or sneaked into the nearby cemetery for tackle football on its front lawn. I couldn't imagine a happier childhood, or better teachers of English and the American way.

Generally, we were very happy with our neighbourhood. When not playing in the street, I'd go to 'block parties' our street held for various Second World War causes. Dad might wander by but didn't join in their draught-beer fests. 'We're not that American,' he'd say, his way of showing disapproval.

All went well until a kid – I don't know who – knocked on a window during our Passover services one evening. It brought my father to the front door; the kid, or several, had run away by then.

I lowered the window shades on the second Passover night but Dad made me raise them. Sure enough, our window was tapped again. This time my father reacted by opening the door, shouted angrily into the dark and so making the trouble-makers happy. Again, he insisted the shades remain up; we weren't disturbed further.

It all bothered me less than when kids recited, 'Matzos, matzos, two-for-five, that's what keeps the Jews alive.' Or when an older kid told me, as a compliment, 'You're a good Jew, Felix, not like some.'

At a time when American Nazis paraded in Manhattan's Yorkville, it wasn't too bad – and I could always find solace practising on the baby grand piano we'd managed to ship with us somehow from Vienna.

Dad did provide embarrassing moments in Manhattan. To my shame, when he spoke German with my mother I'd walk on the other side of the street to distance myself. Didn't they know there was a war on? It got worse – louder – if they walked with other German speakers.

Only if they went to Éclair, a café with great Viennese pastries, did I relax among this refugee crowd. He could still embarrass me, studying every check for mistakes, and finding quite a few. But if a mistake was in our favour – charged too little – he'd point that out too. He also showed class by never seeking a better table. Seated behind a pillar next to the kitchen? Fine, food will be warm when it comes.

Three years after the war ended in 1945, we became real Americans. My father bought a much-used 1937 Pontiac, whose bald tyres often went flat. Our Sunday explorations by bus had turned stale: Dad's desire for a bus ride to rustic-sounding Laurel Hill landed us at the local mental hospital. It gave us a good laugh, but the rust-mobile arrived soon after.

Thinking again about all those trips makes me now recall the later journeys taken with my own family. We might have belonged among those 'Happy Families' until I destroyed that by moving out suddenly at a time Ted has recalled so movingly.

My father wouldn't have acted as I did, or as hurtfully. He would have been immensely pleased that Ted named his son Joseph, after him. But he couldn't have been prouder, or more honoured, than I was.

Felix Kessler is a writer and editor. He worked at the *Wall Street Journal*, as well as at *Fortune* and *Bloomberg*. He has four children, of whom Ted is the eldest.

ACKNOWLEDGEMENTS

Like Communism, or water polo, *My Old Man* has been a purely collective endeavour. If it had been just me at work on this, the enterprise would have stalled with one lonely blog posting about my dad in July 2013. I must first, therefore, thank all who contributed to the My Old Man blog, those whom I cajoled into doing so and those who volunteered their stories as its word spread. The site completely surpassed my meagre expectations for it and grew into a heart-wrenching bi-weekly bulletin into which I had next to no input beyond hosting it. In order of appearance, thanks and praise goes to:

Keith Cameron, Anna Wood, Niall Doherty, Victoria Segal, Andy Capper, Eamonn Forde, John Aizlewood, Mathew Horne, Nick Duerden, Michael Hann, John Mulvey, Roy Kelly, Kieran Yates, Mic Wright, Yasmin Lajoie, Emma Anderson, Fiona Sturges, Anna Parkin, Paul Connolly, Harry Borden, Terri White, Kate Murray, Ellen Storey, Brian Ellis, Jim Butler, Andy Fyfe, Juanita Stein, Michael Tierney, Amanda Freeman, A.W. Wilde, Lisa Edwards, Jim Owen, Jez Kay, Leah Wilson, Jude Rogers, Jacqueline Downs, Dominic Utton, Karen Bevan,

James Firkins, Sophie Van Kelst, Catherine Anne Davies and Mark Townsend.

I started the blog as a hobby, inspired by the nature website Caught by the River, which is run by my friend Jeff Barrett. I hoped that as with CBTR, My Old Man would simply be a place where people could step out of the everyday grind and write about something personally fundamental. I'd like to thank my agent Kerry Glencorse at Susanna Lea Associates for suggesting there could be a book in it and for making that happen, as well as for her wisdom thereafter. And to my brother Mark for offering good counsel when Kerry was on leave.

I offer particular gratitude to Kerry for introducing me to Jenny Lord, my editor at Canongate. Jenny's know-how, encouragement and insight have been invaluable, and I envy the next person to be edited by her. Thanks, too, to Jamie Byng and his amazing address book, to everyone else at Canongate for their work and to my eagle-eyed copy-editor, Hazel Orme.

Rolling this ball up the hill took a lot of hands, so not only do I have to thank heartily the book's contributors for delving so fearlessly into the personal, but also all those who convinced people to contribute, made introductions or, in the case of my Q colleagues, Niall Doherty, Chris Catchpole and Paul Stokes, interviewed Chris Martin, Rod Stewart and Shaun Ryder respectively. I'm very grateful to those who facilitated contributions, including Ben Ayres, Moira Bellas, Ted Cummings, Ruth Drake, Baxter Dury, Susie Ember, Laura Martin, Arlene Moon, Mairead Nash, Jamie Oborne, Marguerite Peck, Scott Steele, Sophie Williams and Jamie Woolgar.

I'd like to thank all those who've appeared at live My Old Man interviews and events with me, particularly John Cryer MP, Peregrine Eliot, Travis Endeacott, Martin and Paul Kelly, and Ben Watt. I tried to make the transcripts work for the book but couldn't capture their in-the-flesh magic.

Finally, I offer thanks and love to my family for generously allowing me to share my version of our story: my partner Jean Coffey for putting up with the long-haul *My Old Man* distraction so stoically, my children Jagger and Joey, my brothers Mark and Daniel, my sister Gaby, my step-parents Jair Kessler and Jim Meyer, and, above all, my dear dad Felix for being such a good sport about it all. God forbid my children pull the same stunt on me.

LIST OF PICTURES

Ted and Felix Kessler, Greece, 1971

Nick and Johnny Ball, dinner 1981.

Tim and Matthew Healy, early 1990s.

Mike and Amy Raphael, London, 1967.

John Niven with his parents, in a caravan, in Scotland, 1967.

Jemima and Ian, The Vicarage, Wingrave, 1973.

John Hamper, 1967.

Rob and Rod Stewart, having a kick-about a long time ago.

Tam Doyle, Filey Beach, Yorkshire, 1974.

Adam and Leonard Cohen, 1977, taken in the kitchen of the Cohen family home in Hydra, Greece, by Adam's mother Suzanne Elrod.

Charlie and Charlie Catchpole, Heathersett, Norfolk, 1949.

Anna and Barry Wood, Worksop, Nottinghamshire, 1975.

Adrian and John Deevoy, Park Prewett Psychiatric Hospital, Hampshire, 1972.

Nick and Florence Welch, 1987.

Harry Doherty and Eleanor Doherty, Blackpool Pleasure Beach, early 1970s.

Adam Ross, front, with his brother, Eban, and father Howard, Vermont, 1983.

Derek and Shaun Ryder, 1990.

Alfred Downs, 1977.

Terri White, outside her home in Inkersall, nr Chesterfield, 1989.

Anthony Martin and Chris Martin.

Dave and Dorian Lynskey, Malvern Hills, 1982.

Paul and John Weller, "smashed in an airport", 1996.

A dead magpie, held in the hand of Rose Bretécher's father.

Yasmin Lajoie with her father and brother, Knaresborough, North Yorkshire, 1993.

Ben and Roy Castle, outside their house in Gerrards Cross, Buckinghamshire, 1977.

Wally Downes Jr and Wally Downes, 2000.

Tjinder Singh and his junior school chess team.

David Michael Griffiths and Joanna Kavenna, in their garden, Leicestershire, 1970s.

Anthony Monaghan and Thelma Pickles' wedding day, November 28, 1959 at 56 Prestwood Crescent, Knotty Ash, Liverpool.

Allan and Tim Burgess, Borth y Gest, Wales, 1973.

Michael Segal, West Norwood, London, 1945.

Richard and Dave Hawley, 1989, Sheffield.

Lubi Barre and her father, Somalia, late 1980s.

Derek Mulvey's RAF dog-tags, worn during post-war national service in Malta.

Tilda Swinton's father, 2015

Felix and Joseph Kessler, Vienna, Austria, late 1930s.